# CATCH THE SPIRIT
## *Riding the Waves of Life*

## Christian Sørensen

**Celestial Winds**
Del Mar, California

Also by Christian Sørensen

**Catch the Spirit – Flying Through Life**
**The Book of Prayers**
**Good Cents**

**Second Edition**
**Published January, 2001**

Library of Congress Cataloging in Publication Data
Sørensen, Christian C., 1960-
Catch the Spirit : flying through life : Christian C. Sørensen

Includes bibliographical references
ISBN 0-943172-89-6 (pbk.)
Spiritual life. 2. Flying—Miscellanea. 3. Self-actualization
(Psychology)—Religious aspects. I. Title.

I dedicate this book to my brother, David
A free spirit, a great teacher of our family,
and my best surfing buddy.

# Acknowledgements

I would like to extend my deepest appreciation,
thanks and love to:

**Kalli,** My beloved wife
who is always there to nurture and support me even
after I have given all to everyone else.

**Marcia Hootman,**
with whom this book would not have been written.

**My Parents,** Reverends Paul and Jackie Sorensen
Who always inspired me to know I could.

**Tina Moreno,**
for her patience in the editing process.

**Rose Sogge, Carolyn Holder, Steve Ostrow**
for Editing.

**Paul Lloyd Warner**
for Typesetting, Book and Cover Design

**And All those people who have allowed me
to serve them through the years of my ministry
at Seaside Church.**


Christian Sørensen
November 2000

# Contents

INTRODUCTION I-VI

1. THE WAVE OF PROTECTION 1

2. SOUL SURFER 19

3. A WAVE OF CONSCIOUSNESS 35

4. IMMERSED IN A WAVE
   OF HEALING 53

5. NO PROBLEM 71

6. A LULL BETWEEN WAVES 87

7. WHAT THE WHALES KNOW 101

8. GOD AND MONEY 121

9. CATCH THE SPIRIT 141

10. BARRELED IN THE WAVE 157

11. EPILOGUE 173

# Introduction

When I first agreed to write *Catch the Spirit,* I didn't think I had any more hours in the day to devote to the task. As a minister of a growing congregation, my time is at a premium. I knew it was important to get my thoughts on paper, but had no idea how the book would unfold.

The next thing I knew my friend, Marcia Hootman, was transcribing away, putting my ideas on paper and tape recording my thoughts on our frequent trips between Los Angeles and Del Mar. I was now finding holes in my day to write, edit and collaborate. I've come to realize how important this work is for me. An energy began to stir inside my being, an energy which has raised its head three times in the past twenty years of my life; an unrest previously provoking me to throw away all the good in my world and run off to chase the waves in some distant land. Today I choose, instead, to use these writings to relive those adventures and remind me that where I am is perfect.

The first bout of unrest came in the late '70s, when I was going to college at the California State University of Northridge. At the time, I thought I was just in the typical rebellious stage of defying the system. I left the traditional educational track behind and ran off to New Zealand with my surfboards and skis in tow. The towering Alps lay less than thirty miles away from the Tasman Sea, off New Zealand's south island. Little did I know, my two favorite sports would be the least significant parts of my adventure.

Heavy storms rolled off the Tasmanian Glacier and pummeled Mt.Cook. Skiing would have to wait until the weather front cleared. I sat by the crackling fire in the recreation room of the youth hostel. Since the weather had kept everyone else away from the hostel, the register was the only other person around.

My eyes moved away from the fire and peered out at the glorious alpine landscape. Paying no attention to the cold, I wandered outside. Amidst the blowing winds, falling snow and pouring rain, there was a mysterious stillness. The now colorless scenery was almost surrealistic, a perfect setting for meditation. I spent several days out in the storms, isolated from the rest of the world, with no diversion. It was my time for deep introspection.

On the fourth day of my lonely wandering, I spotted a river and decided to follow its path. Miles from where I started walking, I noticed a huge boulder with water cascading off its surface like a miniature waterfall. The sound of the rain, the flowing river, the entire landscape and I were engaged in an undeniable unified rhythm. Deep into my meditative state for days, there suddenly appeared before me a bright light at the end of a dark tunnel. I knew the darkness symbolized my life. I also realized now my entire existence was to be about service, the most natural, fluid path of my self-expression would be to serve in the ministry. The plan unfolded before me as a bright, lucid vision. There was no need to think about it or wait any longer. My next step was clear—as soon as I returned to the States, I enrolled in the School of Ministry of the Ernest Holmes College. I had finally found my way.

Years later, while I was tending a growing, loving congregation in Ventura, California in a majestic, old building, with 450 seats, which was designated an historical landmark, the energy of discontent began to stir again. I had done all of the politically correct things in the Religious Science movement. I was a member of our international board of trustees, had a weekly TV show, owned a home on the beach, and was surrounded by loving family and friends. Yet my wife and I threw all this away to chase a dream and follow a rainbow. The dream was to live in Hawaii and start a new work from scratch. Within a few months, we resigned from our prestigious positions on the mainland, put all of our belongings in a cargo container for shipping, placed our cats into their four months of forced quarantine and jumped on a plane to Hawaii.

The church opened in a school cafeteria, but it wasn't long before we were doing well enough to lease our own facility. We owned a spectacular, two-story home, nestled in the jungles of Kaaawa overlooking the beach. Just steps away were the perfect waves for me to surf. By this time our cats had even forgiven us for their jail time.

Three years into this new endeavor, our young, spiritual family was growing, caring, loving and supporting each other when I began to notice that old familiar stirring which felt as if something was missing. It's amazing how this energy rocks the outside world before one realizes it's the inner world where it "takes root" and where it needs to be acknowledged.

Still not recognizing the recurring pattern from within, with very little explanation, I departed the islands that once filled my being and nurtured my soul. I knew the church was in good keeping, for I left it to my wife, who decided to stay. And so once again, I found myself on a plane, this time bound for Indonesia, my precious surfboard in tow. I had abandoned everything I worked so hard to accomplish. In retrospect, I asked myself why my surfboard was the one possession by my side and a new tattoo below the belt line. I had left everything else behind. Why wouldn't I give up this possession? While I didn't consciously know it at the time, my soul knew how important and nurturing surfing is to my spiritual and physical well-being. I know, no matter what's going on in my life, the ocean is one place where I can always reconnect with God.

When you go into what's called a "tube" in surfing, you become one with the wave. Everything outside of you and the wave disappears. You're totally in the moment. Nothing else is relevant. Everyday anxieties are gone. You leave the world behind. Often during meditation you're able to get into the same realm where you sense a oneness with all things, where you know everything feels right. In this place, you can truly "Catch the Spirit." This is the reason my surfboard has been such an important part of my life. To experience the rhythm of the wave, the ebb and flow of the tide, the rough and the smooth sea is to fully experience life.

I share this writing to help you ride the waves of life and to remind myself they exist in everyone's world. If I am feeling there is something missing, it's not lacking in my outside world; it's because I have yet to discover the missing piece inside of myself. It's time for me to catch the spirit within, and this time, stay off airplanes bound for foreign lands. I know Spirit has something extraordinary in store for me, just like it has for each and everyone of us, but you and I have to stay put and give the miracle a chance to take its proper form.

In my search for peace, a comforting vision came to mind. When the Oahu church leased its facility, we painted a phrase above the door that read, "Catch the Spirit." The first day in our new home we asked a local guy and good friend, Clyde Aikau, to perform a traditional

Hawaiian blessing. He came from a lineage of Kahunas serving King Kamehameha, the uniter of the islands. Blessing the facility, Clyde sprinkled sea salt in all the corners of the room to "cleanse away any negative energy," then honored the four directions and the heavens and the earth. We performed the ceremony in order to honor the Spirit in its unique expression of the islands and their heritage. What was interesting was the week the church moved out of the facility, an arsonist set fire to the building and the structure burned to the ground. All that was left was a charred board, which hung above the door with the words, "Catch the Spirit."

Through my dark night of soul searching in my quest for peace, I spoke in various places and waited to recognize my new spot in life. I asked life to give me a sign such as, "What cathedral do you want me to take over?" Nothing showed up. Although the ocean had always been a part of my life, I almost considered looking inland. I didn't have to. Shortly thereafter, I accepted a speaking engagement from a Pamela Kurtz, at a small church in Solana Beach, California.

Sitting in a pre-service meditation, feeling tremendous warmth and love from the small group of twenty-five loyal churchgoers, I opened my eyes and noticed a paper sign hanging above their door. To my amazement, the sign read, "Catch the Spirit." Tingles ran up and down my spine, as I knew that this was the sign for which I had been longing and praying.

Today, I am married to a beautiful, loving woman. Kalli is the soul mate I searched the planet so long to find. I am a minister of a great, spiritual family known as the Seaside Church of Religious Science. The congregation has grown to almost three hundred in the few years I've been here. Things in my world are good, very good. Being where I am brings me immense joy and happiness. Yet, at times those uneasy stirrings deep inside my soul lift their heads and I hear those exotic lands calling. The difference is I now recognize it as an old, familiar pattern I will no longer blindly follow. At this time, I am unwilling to uproot and start again, for the vision I have is grander.

When these recent stirrings came up, instead of searching for a new adventure outside, I acknowledged the unrest and immediately went deep within. My intuitive message was, "Christian, share your story so others may know that the answer is within, not without."

In giving birth to this body of writing, I have once again found the spiritual stance, my place of equilibrium. Spirit has now positioned me for the ride of my life. Come along with me as we "drop in" and *Catch the Spirit!*

Christian Sørensen,
Encinitas, California

# One

# The Wave of Protection

*The power of love can transcend any
challenge.  If we are willing to step into
the consciousness and going to send
the loud signal of love;
it will lift us out of the most
precarious of situations.
When we unite with family,
whether it be spiritual, biological
or extended family,
there is a warmth bringing us from
fear and hopelessness
to courage and trust.*

# Chapter I

# THE WAVE OF PROTECTION

## Neptune, David and Me

It's a glorious December day on the North Shore of Hawaii. I can hear the pounding of the giant waves as they roll relentlessly towards the white, sandy beach on Waimea Bay. The energy of the sea seems to shake every grain of sand. Each person here feels an undeniable, collective magic, an electricity in the air that is not matched anywhere else in the world. Here, with the most powerful of waves, is the place the professional surfing circuit chooses to end its season each year, for this is the birthplace of the sport of surfing.

I can instantly recapture my intense feeling of excitement while catching and dropping in from the top of a 10-foot wave at Raglan, New Zealand. It's easy to envision the beautiful scenery in Bali and its barrels of "Ullu Watu," as well as to picture the perfect tubes of the "Pipeline" or the warm waters of Costa Rica. I can even recall the many times my friends and I cut school, due to what we called "surfing sickness." But some of my fondest memories were of being out there in the "lineup," where surfers wait for the next good wave.

Many of the best conversations I've had with my brother, David, were out in the water, watching and waiting patiently. We talked about our life's direction, our goals and dreams. We discussed brother stuff, like family, friends, partying and, of course, girls. It was during these times of waiting for the next wave I got to know my "crew."

Even at those times when nature was being uncooperative and the waves were flat, my crew was always there. Looking back, I realize just how important they were, not only to my surfing skills, but to my personal and spiritual evolvement.

Surfing, like life, is an individual activity. But when you are frustrated, hurt or fearful, it's so important to know you have support. This is what the crew or surfing family is there for. Just as older siblings take care of younger ones, the more experienced surfers take the newer ones out into the waves. They feel a powerful, unexpressed responsibility to pass on their wisdom, courage and inspiration to the neophytes. I still remember pushing my brother on the surfboard into his first waves.

Nobody can actually teach you the best way to ride a giant wave. Just as with life's lessons, you must learn through your own experience. But it makes the task so much easier when you have people close to you who are supporting, encouraging, urging you to jump right in. Family is our rock, our foundation, and very often, the one, steady light that keeps us going. Oftentimes, family has nothing to do with blood relationship. Families are those who care about you and want to share in your experiences.

I remember watching my brother getting sucked over and devoured by some large waves, just as we all have in life. It hurts inside to watch a loved one crushed by the wave of life. Yet, human beings are amazingly buoyant with our ability to find our way to the surface to ride again. I'd always feel relieved when I saw my brother's head pop up and knew that he was fine. Just knowing someone from our crew is watching is comforting and brings a sense of protection.

## Inspiration

In 1992, a one hundred foot, French Government ship was cruising off the coast of Central Africa. Yanik, one of the crew members, woke up in the early morning and noticed he was sliding down to the front of his bunk. Frowning, he recalled the seas had been calm when he drifted off to sleep. "Perhaps an unexpected storm came in during the night," he thought. Slipping out of the bed, he made his way towards the stairs and opened the hatch. A deluge of sea water poured in, its force knocking Yanik off his feet and rendering him unconscious.

A few minutes later the cook awoke, saw Yanik lying on the floor of the cabin and revived his friend. Taking inventory of their situation, they couldn't deny things looked perilous—by now the water had inundated the whole ship. Fortunately, they were sitting in an air pocket, but more than one hundred feet below the surface. Staring at each other, wondering what they could do, the two men knew they were using up the last of the available air.

They decided to swim over to the hatch and try to pry it open. Yanik pushed with all his strength, but the hatch wouldn't budge. As the hours rolled on, panic set in. The cook went berserk. "This is our tomb. We're going to die!" he shouted.

"Calm down," Yanik advised. "The more panicked you are, the more air you use. And we don't even know how much we have left."

Five hours, then six hours passed; they began to choke from lack of air. Yanik knew they couldn't just sit there and do nothing. He had to come up with a solution—

but what?

Suddenly, a vision of his family popped into his mind. It was as if they were right there with him. After all, there is no distance in the realm of mind. Yanik could see the round, innocent face of his son, Josef, the warm smile of his wife, Risa. He knew that he could not desert them. He had to survive, had to be with them again. And so, uniting with the consciousness of love and support he felt from his family, even in that dark cabin, Yanik decided he was going to try one more time to raise the hatch cover.

Swimming down into the dark, murky waters, he found his way to the opening. The pressure of the hundred feet of water firmly locked the hatch cover in place, but Yanik didn't get discouraged. With the picture of his family still in his mind, and the power of their love and support, a fresh thought came to him: The ship had been out of radio contact with the French Government almost all day. Surely search parties would be sent out. If so, they would be listening for signs of life. Yanik had to find something that would make a loud noise.

Looking around, he spotted a fire extinguisher on the wall and pulled it down. He swam back over to the opening and began to hit the hatch cover with the heavy equipment, pounding as hard as he could. Within a few moments he heard noises from the other side. He had been right! There were divers on the outside pounding back. The rescuers rushed an air tube down so the sailors had enough oxygen. Shortly thereafter, both men were raised up and out of their watery tomb. Although it had been the divers who had saved him, Yanik knew the idea of his family gave him the inspiration to keep going.

The power of love can transcend any challenge. If

we are willing to step into the consciousness and to send the loud signal of love, it will lift us out of the most precarious of situations. When we unite with family, whether it be spiritual, biological or extended family, there is a warmth bringing us from fear and hopelessness to courage and trust. Allowing those difficult times to control your feelings and actions and you have given away your power to the outside world. Instead, choose to honor the Spirit and you will be given the tools to overcome any situation. This is the way of protection coming from the elder of the crew—God.

## Rite of Passage

Growing up, I noticed, no matter what happened during the day, my dad always came home. As a movie actor, my dad would get thrown off horses and buildings, beat up or shot, but he'd still come home. In one particular film, Clint Eastwood hung him from the gallows. I watched my dad dangle, lifeless, on the screen. But he still came home. The movie Star Trek III: The Search for Spock begins with my dad's face filling the big screen. Soon the Klingons came along and totally obliterated him from the universe. But he still came home. My dad was always there for me. He was indestructible—or so I thought.

Some of the greatest joys I experienced in my childhood were the times hiking and hunting in the woods with my dad and my little brother, David. It's been decades since I've had any desire to hunt, and even back then I knew the most enjoyable part was spending time with the "guys."

During one of these outings, I was walking up a hill

when gunshots suddenly pierced the quiet. More jarring than the sound of those explosions was my dad's cry, "Oh, no!" Running up to the top of the hill, I saw my brother lying on the ground, sobbing. There was my dad, looking stunned, holding his shotgun. David, who had collapsed, spotted me and hollered, "Daddy's been shot! Daddy's been shot!"

One of my best friends had come along on the hunting trip with us. He tripped, his gun discharged and put ninety bullet holes of buckshot into my dad. There I was, 15-years-old, having to make a life saving decision. In retrospect, I feel Dad was initiating me, granting me my passage into manhood.

I had no choice but to act at this time. This was real life, not a scene from a Hollywood movie. Here was my dad, no longer the indestructible guy who came home from the studios, day after day. I saw him as the vulnerable human being he was, shot with real bullets, blood spurting out over the ground. Now it was my turn to take charge and get my dad from the country to the hospital. I had been given the opportunity to step from innocence to awareness. Life's wave of protection welled up inside. The elder's energy transferred into an action of knowingness and I performed

Flashing within me, was how grateful I felt for what my dad taught me: Like it wasn't so important to get the part in "Charlie and the Chocolate Factory." Another actor beat me out in the screen test. Dad made sure I knew I was still loved. At baseball games, he taught me about accepting the consequences of my actions. He never lectured me about devouring all the junk food I could at the game. He'd let me buy the two hot dogs, peanuts, cracker jacks and cokes, then quietly hand me a couple of antacid tablets. He was the one who gave me my love for the ocean. He showed me how beautiful the sunsets were, how to find the big and little dippers in the sky and how to build bonfires.

Of all the things my dad taught me, the lesson I needed to remember that day in the woods was the most important. He assured me there was a Fatherly Presence inside of every person on this earth. He said, "We all have access to the Presence. It is there to guide us through challenges, to hold our hands and give us strength. All we have to do is call it forth."

I looked at my earthly father peppered with buckshot, and knew I had to turn to the Fatherly Presence inside of me. "What should I do?" I asked. The answer came swiftly. The three of us helped Dad into the van. Then, I climbed behind the wheel and drove down the winding, country roads. It didn't matter I was a whole year away from getting a driver's license. In fact, I was desperately hoping a police car would pull me over and escort us to the hospital. But in the thirty-minute drive, not one police car appeared.

Arriving at the emergency room, we brought my dad in and told the nurse what happened. "We'll take care of him," she informed me all too nonchalantly, "but first we need these admission papers filled out."
"But my dad's been shot. He needs to see a doctor right now!" I pleaded.

She dismissed my request as the hysteria of a 15-year-old. However, after a few minutes she realized how serious the wounds were. The papers got too bloody to read and Dad passed out on the floor; only then was he given a bed.

An old, "back-woods" country doctor came in and began pulling out the buckshot, one at a time. Just like the movie heroes he portrayed, Dad winced but remained brave. After a dozen pieces of shot were removed, he stood up and announced, "That's it. We're going home!" There's my John Wayne dad for you. Of course, you don't ever want to try and smuggle anything on him at an airport if you're traveling with him. With all the remaining buckshot in his body, the metal detector goes off every time.

Arthur Ashe, the great tennis champion, wrote his memoirs, Days of Grace, shortly before he died. He dedicated a part of the book to his five year-old daughter, Camera. He wrote, "...when you feel sick of heart, or weary of life, or when you stumble and fall and don't know if you can get up again, think of me. I'll be watching, smiling and cheering you on."

Through the horrifying experience of my dad's hunting accident, I was able to really feel the Presence inside of me. I knew that no matter where my dad went, there was always a Father for me to call upon. A comforting wave of protection will follow me all the days of my life.

## Moms See Potential

God created dads because life doesn't come with instructions. Moms were created because God couldn't be everywhere at once. Fathers teach you strength. Mothers look out for you while you're trying out the muscles. They soothe your skinned knees and know the right words to help mend a broken heart. Having the masculine energy in your life is essential. It shows you how to get things done, but it's also important to be able to feel that great cosmic hug, to crawl up into the maternal embrace and know everything's going to be all right. Moms seem to know instinctively.

In India, the wife of an Englishman was in a compound, holding her baby in her arms. Monkeys were not unusual around there, and as she was sitting outside, a big monkey came down and just sat there and watched her hold and nurse her little baby. As the monkey looked at her, she looked at the monkey. Then the monkey took off and climbed up into a high tree nearby and came back with her own little baby and sat down, and the two of them just held their babies.

A mother's love is so simple and pure, something so natural it expresses across all cultures.

I visited Russia during the first years it opened up to the West. While there, I noticed lines of people wrapped around the block. When I asked my guide what the line was for, he responded, "What line?" Later, I found out it was a bread line. I had noted it was made up mostly of women. I heard an interview with an interpreter speaking to one lady wrapped in her coat with a scarf over her head. They were talking about these bread lines and how towards the end of the day, oftentimes, they'll run out of food and riots sometimes break out. She was asked, "Why do you do this?" Her answer was very simple, "I have two children." Because of the two children, she was willing to stand in line for hours. The things moms do for us are amazing. Yet, it's a very natural experience; it is Spirit expressing.

When we were young, my brother and I had a big pine tree on our front lawn with a bunch of flowers growing under it. My mom's godmother, Marie, lived at our house and helped take care of things. She had this beautiful flower garden filled with gardenias. People in the neighborhood loved it. My brother and I would wrestle and throw footballs and destroy her flowers on a regular basis. Poor Marie, we would crush her gardenias and she would get so upset. My mom used to say to her, "Marie, remember, we're raising kids, not flowers."

I broke a few windows in my day. I dropped a few plates. (I think that's a boy's job, to break windows and a few other things.) My mother believed what was important was not to break the spirit of the child; not to break the self-esteem of the person who threw the baseball through the window by mistake.

My mom knows I'm not perfect, but even today she doesn't let on. Because of Mom I believe in the Tooth Fairy, the Easter Bunny and Santa Claus. She always makes my birthday like a national holiday—just a wonderful expression of the heart.

Thomas Carlisle said, "A man lives by believing something, not by debating and arguing many things." When you choose to believe something; when you choose to believe in a higher power; when you choose to believe it's right to experience love; when you choose to believe in the magic and the wonder there is in life, the surprises and the miracles happen. This is when moments of pain are transformed into a deeper understanding of what is right. My mother always believed in me, and by her belief she taught me to believe.

Human beings are blessed with Divine intuition. Female humans pay especially close attention to their feelings. This is the same intuition that sees the unlimited possibilities in a child. A mother sees her child as the fulfillment of his dreams. She sees through to the innate nature, the Spirit that is inside of everyone of us. A mom may realize her child looks like a "Menehune," but knows he is capable of being a big wave rider.

"When the winter swells unfold with thunder, sweeping clean the buried reefs, the wave is no respecter of persons. See yourself smoothly, fluidly, continuously one with the wave," she'll say, "because some day you'll be out there in the critical section being chased by its breaking edge."

Even if her child replies, "You'll never get me out on one of those days," Mom continues to believe, to know and be persistent. She knows how to hold the dream for her child. No matter how hurtful your actions may be, she sees your potential. No matter how much her heart may ache with whatever pain you're going through, somehow the love stays constant. And feeling the love brings a wave of protection, enabling you to catch the Spirit to the fulfillment of your innate potential.

## Unconditional Love

The sea is fickle, you ride the big surf on the ocean's terms, not yours. One spends his life chasing the waves. Every day of surfing brings unlimited possibilities. The higher the surf, the more excitement you can look forward to. But the more exciting the ride, the greater the possibility of the "wipe out," those times when the wave wins the battle and pulls you under: Those ugly sucking holes from the reef, extreme moments when the thundering crash of the lip explodes on the face of the wave, slapping you against what feels like asphalt, body tingling as you're held under by the first wave of a set; swimming for where you hope the surface is, only to get your head out of the water when a bigger wave initiates you into the "two wave hold down club." The bigger the wave, the longer you're going to be down. When you go under, you try not to lose your cool. Getting wiped out is a part of life teaching you valuable lessons: patience, strength and confidence.

You learn patience, letting the more dangerous waves or opportunities you're not quite in position for pass over you until the right one comes along. When you wipe out, it's instant validation you will make it through the turbulent times because you did. In life a challenge may last days, weeks or years. In the ocean the wave swamps you for a few moments and then you recover. Getting back on your feet time after time gives you more strength and confidence than you've ever had before. It takes both experience and fitness for your ability to develop—that doesn't happen from the shore.

It's important not to lose your head and to realize you'll survive. You may drink a little water and be held down by forces stronger than you, but you'll come back to the surface. At least, I have so far. Although my crew laughs at me when I get pounded by a wave, I know they are also watching out for me. Just like dad, they've helped me to gain strength and courage over the waves; and like mom, their eyes are always alert. If my crew sensed I was in real danger, they'd be right there to bail me out. Yet not one of them would discourage me from attempting a bigger wave the next time. They want me to succeed—to accomplish more today than yesterday. They know the wipeouts I go through today will help me with my sequence of maneuvers toward smooth rides tomorrow.

When you begin to buy only into the pain and challenges of life, you lose sight of your vision. A crew of people close to you keeps you focused on what is possible. Achieving your goals and dreams should be as much a desire to you as grasping the next breath of air. Don Quixote, the title character in Cervantes' novel, says, "When life itself seems lunatic, who knows where madness lies? To surrender dreams, this may be madness. Too much sanity may be madness. And the madness of all—to see life as it is, and not as it should be."

## Family is Supportive

In his book, Illusions, Richard Bach tells us, "Rarely do members of the same family grow up under the same roof." Some of us are fortunate and have grown up with a loving family. Many people don't have the opportunity to experience such love, so they look to an outside group to connect with. The important question is, to what and to whom have you connected?

We hear of gangs on the streets of our cities today and think it's a new phenomenon. But even back in the 1950's, an age of more innocence, a popular Broadway show and movie, West Side Story, told a similar tale about two rival gangs, families for kids who felt they didn't have one. Their loneliness drove them to hook up with a group that told them what to think and how to act. Supportive families, on the other hand, allow you to be who you are and respect your opinions and authentic expression.

Tony, the lead character, started a gang called the Jets. They were kids born in New York City. The Sharks, led by Bernardo, were Puerto Ricans. Each gang was held together by prejudice, violence and a thought that they had a particular turf to defend.

As Tony grew and evolved, he could no longer defend the gang's position. He felt there was something better coming, something more. He said, "There's a miracle coming. I don't know what it is, but it's going to be great!" That evening Tony found Maria, the sister of Bernardo, a Shark. Instant electricity surged between them. Had Tony outlined his prayer, telling Spirit, "Here's exactly what I want to happen," he wouldn't have chosen Maria. After all, she was from a different gang, a different family.

Tony and Maria tried to step away from the old. They began to realize that the Sharks and the Jets served no good purpose. They only supported conformity, violence and prejudice. There was no father to teach wrong from right, nor was there any maternal embrace that said, "Everything's going to be okay." The old was no longer an appropriate model, yet it was attempting to suck them back. Vision at this time has to be strong enough to pull one out of the old way.

The story ends in tragedy, like any good Romeo and Juliet archetypal drama. Tony and Maria's love stayed constant, but the warring gangs become victims of their own violence. As Bernardo and Tony are killed, the lesson is clear: Love begets love and violence begets violence.

Be watchful with whom you connect. Is it an energy sending you back over the falls, or one launching you forward for the ride of your life? There are positive connections, such as church groups, sports groups, support groups and charitable organizations. Then there are negative connections: groups who want to control their members, violent protesters, gangs, criminals and scam artists. Stay away from people who show destructive tendencies.

Remember, you are known by the company you keep. When was the last time you looked at your crew? One's crew changes over the years. There are always new friends to paddle into life's adventures. Through positive connections with people you establish deep, intimate relationships, you create a history of your personal and spiritual evolvement. They know who you truly are. They've seen your bad side and love you anyway. They embrace your good side. Everyday they encourage you. When you've wiped out and could use some comfort or when you hurt, you can always come to them or they call you out of the blue. Even when years have passed and you've been separated by time, there's still instant connection when the voice is heard or memories recalled. They will always be there for you, providing a wave of protection no matter where they may be, because love knows neither time nor distance in life.

*Two*

# Soul Surfer

*I'll tell you a not so
metaphysical secret.
At some level, you are responsible for
everything happening in your life.
This is the bitter pill of
New Thought, which is really
an old story.
Yet realize, resiponsibility is a gift
not a burden.
If you accept responsibility for negatives
in your life, you also have control
to produce positive outcomes.
A bitter pill may not taste good going down,
but the results could be great.*

# Chapter 2

# SOUL SURFER

The ocean was always in my future. Spending summers growing up on the beaches of Malibu with two beach-folk parents, I guess the fact was inevitable. One Christmas, mom and dad gave me a big, long surfboard. We'd take it down to the water, sit my six-year-old brother, David, on top of it, and push him along the coastline. We had fun, but my 11-year-old mind was thinking "go-cart," the craze was sweeping the entire neighborhood.

I wanted a go-cart more than anything. My parents finally bought one for me and I began racing around the neighborhood—too fast—and, at times, followed by police cars. A thought occurred to me, "Maybe this go cart wasn't such a great idea." It also didn't take me long to discover I had neither the talent nor desire to work on greasy, mechanical things. More and more I thought about surfing. After all, there wasn't much you had to do to a surfboard: keep it waxed, don't run into piers and, when you want an adventure, just throw it into the back of the car and drive down to the beach. Maybe this was Spirit's way of getting me to follow my true love and get my body into the cool, healing waters of the Pacific.

If there is something in life you are meant to do, the universe will find a way to get you there. Very often, the way is not of our own choosing.

Baby eaglets are forced to learn to fly. Mother eagles, in wanting to sever the dependence tie, demolish their perfectly comfortable nests. Nature purposely makes marsupial pouches only in size small. When the infant kangaroo outgrows the pouch, he has to jump out and, in so doing, gains his independence.

The loving Spirit says, "Go," and so do loving parents. What an amazing oxymoron. Nurturing families are supposed to be there for their offspring, protect them from harm. Yet parents must encourage their children to go forth and discover their own world. Maybe this is why we are watching this "boomerang kid" phenomena.

In today's society, many young people continue to live in their parents' homes well after they have finished school and entered the job market. They find a safe, inexpensive environment easier to handle than going out into the world. There comes a time when we all have to grow up and be on our own—a time to leave the safety of the shore and find our true soul's ability. This is when you find your style and make adjustments to the different pitches of life's waves.

One of today's popular processes in some therapy groups is the symbolic disowning of parents in order to finally sever the umbilical cord. I don't believe you need to go to this extreme. You do need to sever the tie in consciousness so you know you are a free, whole entity. Then you can be someone who can go into any subsequent relationship as a whole person, rather than a needy, half-being, looking for your other piece.

Parent-child dependency and subsequent independence is something that's a natural part of the evolutionary process. Sometimes it doesn't happen until the age of 20, or even into middle age, but it needs to be done. The separation is what allows us to be free and make our own choices about the world. If we let our parents excessively influence us, we end up blaming them when things go wrong. Isn't it a bit strange to think of a middle-aged person blaming their parents for their behavior today?

## Accepting Responsibility

Many people go through their lives blaming others for every negative experience. Our society is in an era which blames the parents. Everything is their fault. Watch the talk shows or the evening news on TV:

"I committed the crime because I was abused when I was a child."

"I can't trust men. My dad didn't love me."

"I don't deserve going to jail. I was drunk when the robbery occurred."

"I'm 35 and overweight because when I was a baby, my mom fed me too much."

"I wasn't driving while I was intoxicated. The accident happened because of my migraine headache."

"I shot the woman because the Twinkies made me crazy."

"I'm a drug addict because my parents were addicts."

I'll tell you a not so metaphysical secret. At some level, you are responsible for everything happening in your life. This is the bitter pill of New Thought, which is really an old story. Yet realize, responsibility is a gift not a burden. If you accept responsibility for negatives in your life, you also have control to produce positive outcomes. A bitter pill may not taste good going down, but the results could be great. Effect follows cause as surely as night follows day, or high tide follows low. If you want to experience healing, or simply live life to its fullest, now's the time to swallow the pill and accept responsibility. This honors your soul, and allows you to surf with the currents as opposed to fighting the rip tides.

Otherwise, you and I live within the invisible barbed wire of the concentration camp of our own mind. And the imprisoned mind throws out little hand grenades of words, inflicting wounds upon the other relationships that happen to come into our world, because the last one was not complete. Unless we let go of previous hurts and resentments, allowing them to be washed away, we will continue to relive the relationships of the past today. The people may look different, but the situations will be the same.

Roy Croft, in one of his well-known love poems, suggests that a truly committed couple can work things out in a more positive way than repeating old patterns. He says, "I love you because you are helping me to make, of the lumber of my life, not a tavern, but a temple. And out of the works of my everyday, not a reproach, but a song."

Relationships give us the opportunity to delve deep inside of ourselves and develop our soul's unique style of expression. So often people move from one relationship to another within very short time frames. This pattern has been labeled, "The Addiction to Attraction." Marianne Williamson compares relationships with drug addiction. She says initially comes the exhilarating high of the first few months, filled with excitement, joy and passion. Then, as the couple gets more comfortable with each other, some human flaws begin to show. Each of them begins to realize their partner is not absolutely perfect, and so they break apart, crashing down from the high, while wondering what happened.

What happened is neither one of them paid attention to what was really going on. Remember this well. People always give you clues. Within the first fifteen minutes after meeting someone, you know if they're sincerely interested in you or if they just want to play games. And sometimes it's just fun to play games and surf with someone different than your crew for a while. But the weather doesn't have to get nasty before you come in, or the relationship doesn't have to get bad before you leave.

To experience the bliss of the ride one must move beyond the terrestrial fiction of perfection, going below the surface of the sea of life to discover their soul surfer. This soul surfer instinctively knows how to consistently maneuver through the critical part of the wave. Part of us wants to accept the fairy tale of love at first sight; or part of us may want to believe that every wave is perfect. What keeps people from delving down below the surface is a lack of belief in the magnificence of our being, so we settle for less than we deserve. Or it could be we feel hungry for the love we never got from our parents, so we're willing to hang onto an illusion. Then we end up disappointed when our dream turns into the same nightmare, over and over again.

Put the videos of your life in reverse, view them again. Which patterns are you continually rerunning? What is it you seem to be committed to: abandonment, control, loneliness, abuse, submissiveness, or dead-end relationships?

There are friends who tell me that superficial relationships are more exciting, romantic and passionate, particularly with people who are unavailable. "The women/men who are available are so dull!" they claim. This kind of excitement is safe, because they know it will end soon. As long as the relationship is temporary, you can be a contender or pretender, there's little danger you'll accidentally reveal your true self.

In my garden, I grow roses. I've contemplated how the beautiful blossoms are like the first blush of romance. Though exciting and wonderful, the blossom can't last forever. Many people lose sight of the fact that the stem, while not as beautiful as the blossom, is necessary to the life of the rose. The rosebud withers and falls off. You can throw away the whole plant or continue to nurture the stem. If you do water what's left, the season will come around again and the romance, the bud, will return. But you must be committed enough to explore beyond the frivolous, initial passion.

### In Love We Trust

Before I met my wife, Kalli, I said I wanted a person I could be honest and intimate with, someone to whom I could safely reveal my soul's deepest secrets and desires. Then she appeared. The very thing I said I wanted scared me more than anything. Here was a woman who allowed me to be open, honest and express my feelings. A healthy relationship is there to assist you to expand and move beyond your fears. When you are fully committed, part of the healthy relationship will be someone who can and will push your buttons, moving you beyond the limits of your previous boundaries.

It's pretty frightening to come to a true realization of your beingness. This happens only when your inner strengths and weaknesses are revealed by an intimate, long-term relationship with another person. The masters and the mystics teach us there is as much inner space as there is outer space. There is as much, if not more, of your being hidden under the surface of your persona as there is showing to the outside world. Are you willing to allow those defenses you have built up through your life to be dissolved?

Alan Cohen's writings reminisced about one of our most famous performers, Jimmy Durante. The old-time actor and comedian had a television show during the 1960's. Each week he would end his show the same way. The stage was dark except for one spotlight directly on him as he sang his closing number. When the last words of the song faded, so did the spotlight. But as soon as the light went off, he'd take two steps toward the side of the stage and right into another waiting spotlight. He repeated this three or four times, until, when the last spot went off, Jimmy took two steps and was off the stage.

Sometimes the light in our love seems to fade. If only our souls could truly believe that the next spot will be there waiting for us, we can let loose of the fear and trust more. If we stay poised for disaster, the indecision creates tension and a wipe out is inevitable. It is as if we were sitting in a car, putting our foot on the gas and the brake at the same time. We want to move forward and open up, but at the same time we're fearful, so we stop. When we put on our commitment brake, we allow room for doubt and fear to replace trust.

In surfing "dropping in" is a term for a place where your trust is absolutely challenged. You're right on top of crest of the wave, looking down the face of it. It's like being right at the very edge of a breakthrough in a relationship, where the choice is yours. You either push yourself into the new experience or walk away.

It's okay to rest on the crest of the wave for a moment—it can be a great, elevated perspective to see out from—but it takes one last, conscious effort, one extra paddle to commit and push in, then you drop in a freefall. You're very clear and focused as to where you're going and the board goes with you, to support you. In life, when you're at the edge of a peak experience, you have to consciously push yourself in. With the push comes the risk, the danger of falling. But with the push also comes the opportunity for success, fulfillment and wonder.

You're looking right down, and it appears as though all the water is being sucked out of the ocean. The bottom of the wave is a long, long way down. In spite of your apprehension, you have to maintain a high level of trust during your freefall. Whenever you lose faith, for even a moment, you turn your power over to outside forces. Allow fear and doubt to enter while you're "dropping in" and you'll get thrashed about by the ocean. Mistrust and lack of faith in a relationship always leads to trouble as well. What's the alternative? It doesn't matter whether your relationship is to the wave or to another person, the alternative is unshakable faith and total commitment to the elevated perspectives of your soul's dreams and goals.

## A Sticky Situation

There's a story of a research scientist for the 3M corporation who was given orders to invent a new kind of paper glue. This paper would stick to any surface you wanted to attach it to, but you had to be able to remove it without injuring the surface. In other words, the company wanted a glue that stuck but didn't stick. The scientist diligently worked on the concept. Months and months passed but he could not find a solution for the challenge. His boss said, "That's enough. We've spent too much money and time without getting results. Let's go on to another project." Something within the scientist's nature knew such a glue was a possibility. So, on his own time, with his own money, he continued the research. Finally, he found the solution. He created what are now called "Post-Its," those little "stick-ums" you find in every office. He wasn't willing to give up when things didn't appear to go his way because he was totally committed to his goal. Are you in tune the rhythm of your soul enough to know that what appears to be a "dead end" is not?

**Unlimited Possibility**

Dr. Martin Luther King's relentless dream was to see all people free. He seemed to know that he wasn't going to be alive to see the day arrive, but it didn't matter. In his final speech, he said, "I may not get to the promised land with you, but our people are going to get to the promised land. I want to do the will of God...That is when all people, of all nations, of all races will join hands and say, 'We are free. We are free. We are free.'" He was totally committed to his goal, regardless of the cost to him personally. It was Dr. King's commitment and his passion for the cause that ensured success. Be willing to be in alignment with the flow, an outlet for its energy, and you will find the flow taking you on the ride of your life to the promised land. Chasing dreams has the probability of taking you over the edge.

**Planetary Love**

History has given us many heroes like Dr. King,

who committed their lives to their love of people from all parts of the world. Not until the last couple of decades has there come a soulful cry to love and care for our planet earth in the manner of respect, such as the indigenous people of undeveloped lands. We have come to realize we cannot continue to abuse our environment and expect the world to survive. We cannot continue to cut trees and remove mountains simply because we want to put a road where they stand. Following are some eye-opening statistics from 50 Simple Things You Can Do to Save The Earth, and the Earth Journal:

~ If the present killing rate continues, nearly all of Africa's elephants will be gone.

~ Each year, 27 million acres of tropical rain forests are destroyed. Ecuador has lost 95% of its coastal forest, threatening 2500 species with extinction.

~ It takes an entire forest—over 500,000 trees—to supply Americans with their Sunday newspapers every week.

~ The average American (with packaging, grocery bags and other paper products), uses the equivalent of 7 trees every year.

~ More than half the cities in America will exhaust their landfills. Already, rising mountains of trash rise high above the ground.

~ In less than two centuries, human (activities) have increased the total amount of carbon dioxide in the atmosphere by 25%.

~ The hole in the ozone layer, caused by motor vehicles, power plants and oil refineries, has now crept over the entire North American continent.

~ The formerly huge Aral Sea in central Russia has nearly disappeared. Due to diverting water for irrigating cotton farms, the sea has already lost more than 66% of its volume and 40% of its area.

~ Norwegian whalers, in the North sea, accidentally kill hundreds of seals each year. Dolphins and other marine life are in constant danger from drift nets and tuna nets.

In his book, Earth in Balance, Vice-President, Al Gore wrote, "Civilization is a powerful, natural force, like the winds and the tides. Our voracious consumption of the earth threatens to push it out of balance."

Does your soul ache when you open your eyes to these facts? It is easier to pretend you don't know this is happening to our planet? Too many people would rather choose convenience over a little change to their life style in order to support the natural rhythm of the life of this mother earth.

Just a few years ago, the first earth summit took place in Rio de Janeiro, Brazil. People from all over the world met to discuss how to save the planet. This consciousness, the one that tells us we are all in this together, will be our saving grace. A new level of world citizenship is essential for our survival on spaceship earth. A heightened awareness of responsibility, inter-dependence and partnership is also important. We must all take a part in restoring health to our environment, and we need to realize the task has to be important to every living being in the world.

Surfing is one part of my life that keeps me connected to other places and other people of the world. As soon as I got my driver's license, my brother and I frequently drove down to Mexico to chase the waves. At 18,

I moved to New Zealand. I've surfed in Indonesia, where you can spend hours without seeing more than two other people, spent time in the liquid lounges of Costa Rica, and lived in Hawaii, the birthplace of the sport, where you can meet the top pros in the world. I became friends with New Zealanders, Costa Ricans, Balinese, Hawaiians and Hispanics. Waiting in the lineup for the next wave, we had some deep, philosophical discussions or just shared some smiles. There I learned about the personal, political and environmental challenges of their various countries. We commiserated about how badly each civilization treats the environment. I became more and more aware of how surfing gave me an expanding, global family and a common language, all the while taking advantage of the opportunity to enjoy ourselves without harming the land, water or air.

Be a responsible citizen of the planet. Do what nourishes you and also your environment at the same time. Let your soul love your life, your world and yourself. Go wherever you know Spirit is in your life. It may be in the ocean, sitting in a church, running, painting or engaged in music. Wherever your personal pleasure is, whatever makes you cry or feel, take time to reconnect with the rhythm of your soul and the natural good of God.

*Surfer* magazine asked board designer, Skip Frye why he surfed. Skip replied, "...I guess you could say that I go to the ocean in order to see God." Wherever your mind is most peaceful, is where you will reconnect with God.

**Time Out**

Yesterday I was meditating on the cliffs over the Pacific. I watched a huge flock of pelicans gliding along the coast. Out of the line, one dropped off by itself and sat in the water right in front of me. We just looked at each other for a few moments, then he flew out over the ocean.

People who are caught up in the "race" of the human race miss out on the gifts life has to offer. Too often it is only the threat of disease or death that awakens us. It says, "Take a look at your life and remember Spirit is always with you." When you're looking for the soulful connection, realize it's always available. Like a boat running out of fuel, pull into the spiritual dock to fill up. Love is the fuel of your body, soul and heart. What do you love? Are you taking the time to refuel your soul? You can do that by reaching out— you'll find hands and heart to support you.

There are those who are here to offer love. Whether it is as parents, romantic partners, workers, or fellow sportsmen/women, you always have the choice to be willing or unwilling to give and accept love. May you never be lonely. May you always have friends with whom to talk and share. May your soul feel the cosmic embrace around you and tell you, "Everything is okay!"

Become one with the rhythm of the wave of life. Feel the love of the Presence moving through you—the propelling fuel of your being. Feel love in your world. Feel a sense of fulfillment and satisfaction. Love yourself. Practice self-respect. Live your life in a place of integrity, with harmony between your words and your actions. Harmony of your being will make your world whole, right and loving exactly where you are.

Spirit, the life principle, is behind you, supporting, nurturing, urging you forward. Breathe in the divine light and become a shining example of love, fellowship and family. Your soul yearns to ride the cresting potential of your being, the one which will take you over the top.

# Three

# A Wave of Consciousness

*Our philosophy believes as the sages
teach, "As within, so without."
Ideas, thoughts and opinions
eventually take form in our outer
world. It seems negative input fed to us
from the outside is more accessible
than positive input.
Although the media does a masterful
job of keeping us informed, we are blasted
with more bad than good news. One of
these days people will be fed up and no
longer want to believe the angles the news
executives decide to feed us. There will be
a new wave of consciousness, no
longer the effect of the ferocious intentions
of the present critical mass of
negative energy crashing down on us.*

# Chapter 3

# A WAVE OF CONSCIOUSNESS

Bouncing off the rocky bottom of the reef, I scratched my way towards the surface for air, gasping for breath as my head broke the water. Looking around for my surfboard, I began reeling it in by its leash. My brother and I had gone surfing off "C" Street in Ventura, and I'd been flying across the face of an overhead wave, when the wave pitched, hurling me into a shallow water wipe out. Now, as my surfboard grew closer, I saw what looked like a heap of kelp dangling over it. But when it got close enough for me to grab, I discovered the kelp was in reality a hideous creature. Yanking back my hand, I stared in wide-eyed horror at the sea serpent clinging to my board. (Okay, it was an octopus, but it might as well have been a sea serpent as far as I was concerned.) It seemed to have staked its claim—to my surfboard! Cautiously gripping two edges of the board so as not to touch the slithering mass, I tried to shake the slimy entity off. It didn't budge—ironic, because as another wave assailed me, I sure did. Being in the "impact zone," where the waves are continuous, I knew the ocean wouldn't grant me any calm stretches to make settling my little property dispute a stress-free process.

I clawed for the surface again—again spitting out saltwater and swallowing gulps of air—and again reeling in the leash to find the creature still wrapped in place. A new tactic was in order. Gingerly, I attempted to pluck the animal off tentacle by suction-studded tentacle. Another crashing wave put a tumultuous end to that strategy (which hadn't been meeting with any great measure of success).

This time when I returned to the surface, I saw my brother paddling towards me. Momentarily relieved, my heart swelled with hope and gratitude. Sudden sentiment filled me—my little brother had come to rescue me. Imagine my frustration when David eyed the situation and threw back his head in laughter. He then paused just long enough to call out, "Hey, scuba man!" before he paddled off to catch his next wave. (Of course, he didn't realize how dire my situation was. In his defense, I must point out that as his "big brother" not only does he tend to see humor in my predicaments, he also tends to think I can handle any that come my way. Many times I find his unwavering confidence quite touching—but this wasn't one of them.)

My near rescue took place just seconds before yet another wave battered me. When I panted to the surface, I grabbed one end of the board and threw my legs around it, using my feet to try to push the octopus free. I actually had it half way off when the next set knocked me off the board and back under water to skid painfully across the treacherous reef.

Flaying my way towards the surface again, I was totally exhausted. Beaten, I surrendered—I couldn't do this on my own—I turned it over to Spirit. "This is it God," I thought. "It's all yours. I let go to you!" My head finally crashed above water again. Hand over hand, I tugged painstakingly on the leash until my board came into reach of my fatigued arms. Flailing towards it, I collapsed on its surface—only to find the octopus was gone.

Listlessly draped there, my heart pounding, lungs burning and all my muscles screaming, I couldn't help but imagine the energy I might have saved if I had turned it over to Spirit to begin with.

## As Within

When the '92 riots occurred in Los Angeles, I was at a meeting in Sedona, Arizona, with over one hundred other ministers. At 11:00 a.m. a note was delivered to Dr. Dan Morgan. Located on Crenshaw Boulevard, his church was in the heart of troubled south L.A. and Dr. Dan was part of the peace coalition. The next time I saw him, he was appearing on the evening news. All the ministers prayed with him and the rest of the country. One might ask, "If Spirit wants only the best for us, how could a tragedy such as this happen?"

Our philosophy believes as the sages teach, "As within, so without." Ideas, thoughts and opinions eventually take form in our outer world. It seems negative input fed to us from the outside is more accessible than positive input. Although the media does a masterful job of keeping us informed, we are blasted with more bad than good news. One of these days people will be fed up and no longer want to believe the angles the news executives decide to feed us. There will be a new wave of consciousness, no longer the effect of the ferocious intentions of the present critical mass of negative energy crashing down on us.

It seems the purpose of television is to get high ratings so they can charge the advertisers more. That's why talk shows don't feature "Leave it to Beaver" families. Instead, you see siblings who air their dirty laundry in front of millions of viewers. I don't know, but maybe those who tune in feel more optimistic about life when they see someone else worse off than they are. Newspapers are filled with sensationalism because the public doesn't scramble to buy "good news" stories. Some of the most highly rated radio shows are called "shock" programs which strive to get us emotionally involved in a politically charged issue. We get so caught up in the presentation, we forget to investigate its truthfulness. News merges with entertainment, holding the attention of the general public.

The information we take in moves through the filter of our consciousness and is absorbed as reality. We're in an era where people believe that what they see and hear in the media is a natural state of being. Poverty, suffering and crime are the norm. In today's world it's almost impossible to feel happy, prosperous and safe—or so we're led to believe.

As each one of us buys into fear, doubt, negativity or hopelessness, we add more weight to what is known as the collective consciousness. (Nowadays we might rename this the "tabloid consciousness," since this is where much of the sensationalism is reported.) This theory says when enough people believe a certain way, that way becomes the gospel for them. For instance, each decade has brought a new mass fear.

During the '60s, many people built bomb shelters on their properties because they feared a nuclear war and believed a shelter would save them. The '70s showed a proliferation of alcohol and drug rehab centers. Anyone who had more than a glass of wine a day was suspect. Ask any child in the '80s, "What's the biggest problem today?" Their answer was, "Drugs." In the '90s the problem of gang violence has loomed large and terrorism has found its way into our experience. All of this is an effect of our collective consciousness.

This kind of consciousness does not happen overnight, nor is it restricted to events around us. The human body is a microcosmic example for what happens in our world. One day you wake up with a stomachache. Instead of finding out what caused the discomfort, you pop a couple of antacids and the pain goes away. Two months later, the ache comes back stronger. Now it takes several antacids to quell the pain. A year goes by and you may end up in the hospital with bleeding ulcers, or worse. As the body gives us signals, so does everything else in our world.

Just because there is calm on the surface, doesn't mean there is no turbulence below. Just because there is quiet out on the streets, doesn't mean there is no unrest within the hearts. For peace to be true it must be through and through, like a wave one can see rolling across the vast expanse of the ocean. Inevitably, what's going on below will surface.

A body of consciousness screamed out across the country more than thirty years ago. Reading quickly through the Commission's report, one might think the Watts riots happened yesterday instead of long ago. Contrary to popular opinion, the Rodney King verdict was not the cause of the '92 riots. It was only an effect of a long-term symptom not dealt with when it first appeared. Just as our bodies can eventually get our attention, so do terrible events such as riots, looting and beatings.

I neither condone nor support violence for any reason. The end doesn't necessarily justify the means. Yet I remember watching the news and cheering on the people of Yugoslavia, Tienanmen Square, Moscow and South Africa, as they took back their freedom. I recalled traveling through the beautiful countryside of Yugoslavia, and the kind conversations with the people in Russia, having been blinded by the sun, standing in the Lime quarries on Robben Island in South Africa, I was mentally transported back to Tienanmen Square, where I had once stood. "Yes," I thought, "stand up for what is right and just." Truth and justice can come out of chaos—the Berlin Wall is history; Apartheid is no more; Communist rule in the Soviet Union is a thing of the past. Very often in letting go of our "small mind's" way, drastic measures become the only solution.

There is a saying: When God tries to get your attention, he first tickles you with a feather. (The funny feeling you usually ignore, when things don't seem quite right with your job or relationship). Then God gets out a small stick. (You and your partner have a few more spats and the boss calls you into her office one more time.) When you don't pay attention to the first two clues, God takes out the cosmic proverbial two by four. Wham! This could be the bottom line purpose of any disaster. In 12-step programs we often pray for loved ones to "hit bottom." It's Spirit's way of saying, "There's something wrong here. Pay attention!" And we do. After suffering any devastating loss, people come together as never before, Red Cross donations go up, people reach deep into their pockets to give money. A recent phenomenon has been celebrities who put on benefit concerts such as Farm Aid and Comic Relief to raise money for charitable causes, as well as vocalists who record money-raising albums as a group. One of the most famous and successful examples, the recording "We Are the World" raised millions of dollars.

## Was The World Flat

The lesson for us is that consciousness, whether positive or negative, grows slowly and steadily. For most of us, our minds, hearts and souls are fed with what we take in with our senses from the surface. There have been numerous studies on both sides of the argument of whether or not the media affects us. We are dealing with a natural law of cause and effect, thought and form. The "New Thought" movement, which is ancient truth, teaches ideas are created into form. When enough of us share the same opinion, think the same thoughts, or fear the same enemy, our collective ideas will be revealed into form. If we think the 6:00 p.m. news is the way things are, this then becomes our collective experience – often forgetting it's some news executive's spin and opinionated perspective of events.

We can look to metaphysical teachings for the answer. The great teachers tell us, wherever we place our energy becomes more powerful in our lives. They also state, that our thoughts, feelings and ideas are revealed into form.

Top movie actors are given a choice of parts. They carefully scrutinize the scripts and choose those they feel are the most entertaining and riveting. A further consideration is, "Will the public come to see this movie?" Marketing studies show them which types of films have been the most successful. So when our favorite action heroes continue to make shoot 'em up and blow 'em up movies, they arc simply catering to our tastes. They are answering the demands of our collective consciousness. Look at the types of movies Hollywood dishes up—and moviegoers pay $8.00 to go and see.

Of course, there are also exceptions, such as animated Disney films, romantic comedies and a newly emerging phenomenon the collective wave is starting to support, shows with spiritual undertones. But most of the box office hits are action films. Is it any wonder we have seen an increase in bombings and other forms of violence? When we are watching vehicles and people being blown to bits on the big screen, are we not putting too much energy on violence? Critics will even mention the degree of violence in a particular film: "There were only ten people killed in film A, but more than thirty in film B." Do these films affect our children? Research tells us they probably don't see reality in the killings, because they're used to seeing cartoon characters blown up on television every Saturday morning.

We've become desensitized to hearing about death. Traffic fatalities and gang shootings seem commonplace to us. A terrorist bombing that kills many people gets full news coverage in all the media. Yet the murderer who kills one person at a time gets a small headline. Why are we not outraged when even one of us is hurt? It may be that movies, news reports, videos and TV mini-series have put us into a slowly engulfing fog, an illusional stupor. By the time children leave home, they will have seen literally thousands of murders on TV; and who knows how many visual killings they were part of on the video or computer screen, all in the name of learning. There is a collective callous that has become necessary for any kind of feeling person to survive. Yet do we really think we can actually turn on and off our feelings with this numbing process?

Oil companies raise gasoline prices one cent at a time. We hardly notice the increase until one day we realize they're charging ten cents more than last month. Perennial dieters will tell you that they paid no attention to the ounce by ounce gain and suddenly were twenty pounds overweight—again. More and more weeds creep into a garden and one day take over the flowers. We slowly allow ourselves to slip into a spiritual trance, taking in outside suggestions and living them as truths.

On a skiing trip in Park City, Utah, Kalli and I were unpacking when I tuned into the weather forecast. "This is the biggest storm of the season," the announcer said, "it's going to be a cold, long winter."

As we were leaving San Diego the forecaster remarked, "This is the worst rain in a hundred years. It's going to be the longest, coldest winter ever." Last August I heard, "It'll be the hottest summer in recorded history."

Why do weather forecasters and listeners focus on the negative? I love to ski. When I hear about big storms and how long the winter will be I think, "Great, ski season will last until late spring!" A long, hot summer means more beach time. Negative thinking, just like positive thinking, is simply force of habit and habits can be changed. Who are you letting do your thinking?

We accept less than perfect health, holding onto negative thoughts: "I'm just getting my winter cold. I get sick every year at this time." "I always get allergies in the spring."

We believe annual statistics, such as: "Fifty people die in traffic accidents every Memorial Day." "There are two hundred homicides in Washington, D.C. each year." "The hay fever season has begun. Watch out!" Statistics will change when we change.

People get caught up in the wave, rather than consciously going below the collective belief. Our entire culture seems to function in this hypnotic trance. Traffic fatalities and gang shootings are part of everyday living. We expect to hear about murders. We've gotten to the place where this is the norm. Such events don't affect us any more than a cartoon character like the roadrunner blowing up Wiley Coyote again. Listen closely: One gang murder is too much! We pretend it doesn't matter, doesn't concern us. After all, the crime didn't happen on our block. Yet, many of us live in fear, mistrusting others. We put dead-bolt locks on our doors, build walls around our communities for protection, and take self-defense classes. And too many of us decide to become gun owners—just in case. This is a consciousness left over from the pioneer days, one that doesn't belong in today's world.

Many of us know we have the ability to change our outside circumstances. Optimistic people say we can have safe neighborhoods again. Yet most don't believe, declaring, "That's a pipe dream." As long as we buy into the idea that "they" are out to get us, it will be a dream. But if we all do our part by maintaining peace inside of ourselves, within our own families and inside our homes, we can have peace in our outside world, the calm surface reflecting what's below.

Last Mother's Day I was having a conversation with my bass player at church. Winfred told me he and his wife had raised fifty-two foster children and six biological ones. As far as he knew, not one of those kids has ever been in trouble. The interesting thing about this story is that Winfred lives in the part of town where drive-by shootings happen every week and drug dealers hang out on street corners. This family knows, as Eleanor Roosevelt said,

"Water will not get in your boat and sink it unless you allow it to." These foster parents believe their neighborhood is already safe and so do their kids—and so it is!

Recently, a group of American school children visited the former Soviet Union. Upon the kids' departure from Moscow, one young American girl was about to climb up the steps to board her plane home when she stopped to wave to her new found Russian friends, tears streaming down her face. One Russian boy standing near, reached out to wipe a tear from her cheek and place it against his heart. He never learned she was one of "them."

We must free ourselves from thinking, "We live in dangerous times." Now is the opportunity to open up to a new way of being. Instead of the separation of "them" and "us," let's invite our enemies into our camp and share our fears, hopes and dreams. Let's learn from our children and move closer together—not further apart. We are living in a phenomenal global time when there is a collective wave saying, "Differences no longer need to be settled with world wars; we won't do business with nations who practice inhumanity to man." What thinking do you want to be part of, the small gang consciousness that feels it has to defend "its turf" or the emerging global heart that's been growing ever since the end of World War II?

## Growing Pains

At times, tough things happen to good people on a grand scale. When paddling out into the surf, you can sometimes catch waves without even getting your hair wet. Then there are those times when the waves are so big and nasty, looking powerful and ferocious enough to devour you. Even in these times you have an opportunity to exercise free choice. Panic and do nothing and the thundering titanic wall of white water will consume you and hopefully spit you out in one piece (not fun). A better solution is to "duck dive," taking the nose of the board, going underneath the wave, allowing its momentum to pass you by, and come up and out the other side. Situations in everyday life are similar. You can either get sucked in by the challenges, or you can allow the negativity to pass right over your head. The choice of whether to be part of the statistics and law of averages or to live an exciting, beautiful life is all yours.

It's difficult to ignore negativity in an era where we are lulled into believing bad news is the gospel. Remember, we hear only a small piece of the whole—the part we support with our wallets. Although we were put here to celebrate life, somewhere we've wandered off the path of light and embraced the darkness of separation. Unfortunately, it seems it takes a disaster such as a flood, an earthquake, or airline crash for people to come together. Yet relationship is what we must embrace every moment of the day.

World civilization is quickly merging into a gigantic, unified whole. The technology of communication has brought us much closer together. News from across the ocean used to take weeks to reach us. Now we're able to pick up a cellular phone and talk to someone standing in the middle of the African Savannah. Affluent Westerners can no longer deny the existence of Third World peasants. We send protective troops into Civil Wars of nations that were once just a dot on the map to us. As the world population expands, world citizens are becoming more and more interrelated.

We are one organism, closely bound to every other person on this planet. On a scientific level, scholars have told us we share atoms with every other human being, living or dead. The process of breath is a continuous intake, outflow and sharing of human energy. "Blood is thicker than water," is a fantasy. We are all related on a deep, cellular level. Yet we try to distance ourselves from those people who don't look like us or live a different lifestyle. The more we cocoon, the thicker the walls become around our hearts, deadening us to the emergence of the global heart, the collective wave seeking to break upon the shores of each of our souls. In these times of distancing, the universe gets our attention, usually in the form of a flood, earthquake, fire, or mass bombing.

The World Trade Center bombing shocked us; but at least we could take some solace in the fact the alleged perpetrators were Mid-Eastern terrorists and not Americans. Then came Oklahoma City. We watched the horror on TV and asked, "Why?" Maybe the answer lies in the birthing of this global organism we are becoming. Are these birth pains we are going through? If so, this is not the time to ask, "Why?" It's the time to ask, "How can I help?"

As preachers preach, "God is everywhere," their congregates wonder, "Where was God in Oklahoma?" If we truly believe God is everywhere present, He/She is in the midst of disasters. Even in the destruction of the Federal Building in Oklahoma City, the stars continued to shine, the sky was still blue and life went on. We could concentrate on the loss of lives or see God there, in the form of the firemen and even the rescue dogs, frantically sniffing out signs of life.

In his work, The Ultimate Revolution, Walter Starcke talked about the unrest of the 1960's, "...I had to tell myself not to be confused by the violence and disruption." Students were staging sit-ins to protest the war in Vietnam. Citizens burned American flags and walked picket lines. There was an international monetary upheaval with nations manipulating their currencies, so inflation was running rampant. Starcke likened the upheaval to gardening. In order for a garden to flourish, you must cut back some leaves, dig up wilting plants, pull up weeds and replant. Maybe this is what's happening to our society today. Is it just time to rid ourselves of the weeds in our collective gardens of consciousness?

I can't answer the question, "Why?" This kind of intelligence is not in my conscious awareness at this time. Am I angry with the people who bombed Oklahoma City? Of course I'm angry. It would be inhuman not to feel the anger. But my choices are limited by what I wish to add to the collective consciousness of this planet. Do I want to contribute to the hysteria or step back and assist in the healing? I can vent my anger at society or the government, or express sentiments of hate at the perpetrator—but then he may be just acting out energies of my consciousness that I've added to the collective. Could it be we all have some repressed hostility? Is that what you want to add to the collective wave? Or do you want to be part of the healing? Remember, all the thoughts and feelings of our ancestors before us have added to our consciousness. If we accept that we carry some of the same atoms which were present in the body of Jesus and Buddha, we also have inherited particles from Attila the Hun and other historical despots.

Ernest Holmes tells us at the very core of our being, there is a part of God which has never been violated. Below the surface, if we dive deep enough, we will find a calm returning to the surface in a more peaceful state. If we want our world to pour forth goodness, we must choose to see this Presence. Recognize every destructive action as a call for love. We must be the ones to answer this call.

Know, in the midst of the most horrific experience, God is always present. It is our responsibility to stay connected to the precious part within us. To only cry out in anger at the government, society or terrorists would be adding fuel to the fire of hatred. We must step out of the hypnotic, cultural trance and stand instead with Divine Truth. Hug people in times of pain, comfort those who hurt, love those who are in need and behold the world from the eyes of Loving Spirit. Only in this manner will we create the space for healing to unfold. For only love can heal the lack of love.

*Four*

# Immersed in
# A Wave of Healing

*When our minds are in discord,
it's difficult to feel harmony.
When we've got our mind
concentrated on problems, it's tough
to hear God, and healing
is next to impossible.
The mind cannot think two
contrasting thoughts at once, nor can
the body feel two opposite emotions.
How can you be at peace in the same
moment you feel anger? And how can you
expect good when you are thinking negative
thoughts? The waves do not discriminate,
nor does the life force
moving through this world.*

# Chapter 4

# IMMERSED IN A WAVE OF HEALING

Huge, perfectly formed waves curled and crashed across the horizon. They were the kinds of waves every surfer loves to find. Strapping the long rubber leash connected to the end of my surfboard around one of my ankles, I put my board under my arm and trotted out into the water. Carefully gliding my board on the ocean's surface before hoisting myself on top of it, I paddled out to the breakers filled with a sense of anticipation. I sat waiting for my wave and when it came I was off, riding it with all the prowess and skill at my command. The wipe-out seemed to come out of nowhere—one minute I was ONE with my board and the wave, engulfed in a sense of wholeness, the next I was churning in the spin cycle of the wave's fury. In my haste to get my head above water, I was pulled off-course by my leash, which had picked up what seemed to be half the kelp beds of the west coast. Dragged this way and that, my board had become an unpredictable and threatening missile as it bounced between the force of the wave and its tether. In the midst of the confusion of the unexpected events, I felt I was running out of breath and options, but I knew what I wanted—air and freedom. I needed to escape my struggle with the force of the wave and the pull of the weighted leash. Reaching for my ankle, I managed to unfasten the leash. With its release, my sense of wholeness was restored. Again at one with the wave, I was immersed with its flow and allowed its liquid force to carry me to shore, where I found my board waiting for me. The experience brought new meaning to Ernest Holmes' words, "We live a life of wholeness and fulfillment in this world only to such a degree as we are able to enter the activities of the world and not be destroyed by them."

## A Silent Miracle

When we think of a person as "whole" most of us envision someone who has a healthy body and mind, with full use of all extremities. Wheelchair bound people are thought of as disabled. Yet, many stories have been told of so-called handicapped people who overcome outside circumstances and do extraordinary work; immersed in a wave of truth, they are not stuck in the rip tides of limited perceptions. The Special Olympics demonstrate how attitudes are more important than aptitude. There are blind skiers, golfers, skydivers, paraplegic basketball players and mountain climbers. The Nobel laureate scientist from Harvard University, Dr. Stephen Hawking, cannot use his arms, hands or feet, yet his research into the mysteries of the universe is world-renowned. He writes through a computer that responds to the blinking of his eyes. Is he not whole, or would we like to see him healed? Itzhak Perlman, the famous violinist, walks onto the stage on crutches, due to the effects of polio. Is he a whole person? Healing means "to reveal the wholeness in our mind, our body and our affairs and to express life in a wonderful way." Healing, therefore, is not measured by circumstances or physical condition, but by one's ability to enjoy and embrace life. We have no right to judge wholeness by our personal criteria. Wholeness is unique to each individual.

The Seaside Church is located in a community in

the northern part of San Diego County. Every summer thousands of people pour into the town for the summer thoroughbred-racing season. On opening day last year, I heard a radio interview. The celebrity guest was Willie Shoemaker, the "winningest" jockey of all times. Right after he quit the racing circuit, "The Shoe," as he was called, was in a car accident and was paralyzed from the waist down. He is now a horse trainer, refusing to be stopped just because he became a paraplegic. The interviewer was sympathetic to the former jockey's condition. Willie noticed the man's attitude and remarked sharply, "I don't want sympathy. I want a winner." Willie's brand of passion and conviction could pull all of us through any challenge.

Ralph Waldo Emerson said, "Once you make a decision, the universe conspires to make it happen." When we know very clearly the direction we want to go, we are immersed in God's wave of wholeness—we are in partnership with the Divine. This life force transcends the challenge. We need to be very clear about our wants and desires and get out of the way, letting Spirit create the healing.

## Without Words

Several years ago, I awoke one Monday morning and felt a slight pull in my right, inner thigh. I thought maybe I strained it surfing or playing tennis. On Tuesday, the pain was still there; Wednesday and Thursday it grew progressively worse. By Friday, my leg was so swollen with inflammation; I couldn't get out of bed. I had to admit it was time to see a doctor. (Sometimes it takes metaphysicians a little longer to come to this conclusion, forgetting

God is in and through all things, including doctors.)

My appointment was late afternoon. The doctor took one look at the leg and called the radiology lab. Since it was almost 5:00 by then, he had to make a special request to get me in. I hobbled down to the lab, where they slapped me on a gurney and put me through a Star Wars looking tube, the CAT scan machine. Prior to this, I had only seen doctors for checkups. Now I was being put on an electric table and dropped through a hole, where technicians took pictures of my body.

After the test was over, I got dressed and returned to the doctor's office. My x-rays were already hanging on the wall, lined up in a neat row. "Hey, Christian," the doc said, "you've got a tumor the size of my fist, in your lymph nodes. I've reserved a bed for you in the hospital. You need to check in so we can do a biopsy tomorrow to see if the tumor is malignant." These last words weren't ones I ever expected to hear in conjunction with my body.

"There's no way I can do this," I told the doc. "After all, I have church on Sunday." That particular weekend was the kickoff for a yearly program. Fifty volunteers had been planning the event over the last several months. They were counting on me to introduce what we had worked on for so long. "I just can't be there," I repeated.

"You must," the doctor insisted.

"Sorry, doc. I'll see you on Monday," I countered. He knew I wasn't going to budge.

I went home and called some of my spiritual practitioners, my prayer partners, to get more of the healing wave of consciousness going. When you are in the midst of a critical challenge, experiencing pain, confusion or frustration, self-healing can become difficult. During times of pain and fear it's tough to maintain the absolute knowingness that you are a whole, perfect, spiritual being. This is why in our teachings we have a healing group known as Spiritual Practitioners. They are trained in what's called "spiritual mind treatment". The Practitioner's task is to see past any physical or mental manifestation and know the spiritual truth of the one requesting the prayer. The one requesting the prayer is absolutely immersed in a wave of healing. The spiritual truth is I'm already whole; when the physical shows something different the wave is the local motion from the absolute to the individual. I knew there was no way for me, Christian, to do the healing myself. The wonderful part was: I knew I didn't have to; I only had to create the space for Spirit to heal me and get myself out of the way. This began to occur the moment I dialed and reached out for assistance, the moment I cut the leash and surrendered to the Divine currents.

For the next forty-eight hours I perspired intensely, as if my body was detoxifying. Sunday morning, I lay in a prone position until the last moment, crawled painfully out of bed, and left for church. Of course, the topic of the day was "Healing." I'm sure this was no coincidence.

To me, a Sunday service has a certain flow and a building of spiritual energy, culminating in prayer. All the talking is to prepare each person's consciousness to be individually receptive to the healing powers of the Spirit, creating a collective atmosphere for the felt experience. Just as I did every Sunday, I spoke my words and then began my prayer. The first few sentences came easily and effortlessly. Then my vocal chords stopped working, I couldn't get any more words out of my mouth. My eyes began to well up with tears. I knew something ethereal, yet real, was happening.

A few moments passed. Suddenly, as if some heavenly hand stretched down, in front of more than two hundred people, the lump in my leg instantaneously dissolved—gone with no sign of its ever having been there. There I stood, unable to speak, tears running down my cheeks. This was, without a doubt, the loudest silence I had ever encountered. In those few quiet moments, I was unaware of what was going on. Everyone in the church knew they were witnessing something wonderful, but I never mentioned what was going on with me ("show must go on" syndrome). It was one of those rare times where words could not and should not describe the experience. Yet everyone walking out the door said it was my best prayer, I didn't say a word, but they heard – and I wasn't the one they heard.

I later realized what happened—I had simply let go, cutting the leash tethered to my garbage. We are told to, "Let go and let God," but we often get caught up in trying to shape the events of our lives. Many people brought up with a wrathful God believe to let go means they will suffer? As for myself, there were numerous challenges in my world and instead of dealing with them, I chose to remain tough, ignore them and keep a positive mental attitude. Any negativity or criticism that came my way, I pretended to ignore. But the doubts and fears were still there, growing inside of me. Finally, below the surface of my smiling face the swamp of my mind filled up with toxins. They had to come out somewhere, so they appeared in my physical body. In my moment of healing, I made a decision to depersonalize the attacks. The people were not critical of Christian the man, but of Christian, the public person. They would have had the same attitude toward anyone in leadership. The more I'm willing to race up and down the waves of life showing my style and moves, becoming more fluid in my true expression, the more many will relate and many won't.

When my mind let go, so did my body. The remarks made by almost everyone in my congregation were the same; as they filed past me, most of them told me, "Christian that was the best prayer you've ever done." There was no need to remind them that I hadn't said a word!

Human beings think or feel. Words are the most often used tools of communication. If you've ever visited a foreign land where you didn't speak the language, you know how difficult communication can become without words. Yet they also constrain us to only that which we know, whatever we can label. The spiritual realm is far beyond anything we've ever been able to articulate. When we allow ourselves to be immersed in indescribable being-ness, we will experience the ineffable current of Spirit.

The Awesome Power of Prayer

Every Sunday morning, the television airwaves are full of testimonials about prayer. Televangelists all over the country report how people are healed by asking for assistance from a church prayer ministry. We've seen people throw away crutches after experiencing a laying on of hands. But until recently, much of this seemed like a sideshow. Then people like Dr. Larry Dossey came to the forefront. He reported findings of numerous experiments using prayer to test the growth of plants and healing of bodies. His studies showed even bacteria responded to prayer. Now traditional medical science is showing us the power of prayer as well.

More than a decade ago, a cardiologist from General Hospital in San Francisco ran a study of heart patients. Three hundred and ninety-three patients from cardiac arrest units around the country took part. Two hundred names were given to prayer groups all over the country. The other hundred or so were treated medically as usual. This was what is known as a "double blind study." The patients didn't know which group they were in, the nurses didn't know and the doctors didn't know. All they were told was that some people would be prayed for and others wouldn't.

Results were striking. Many patients receiving prayer treatment required fewer antibiotics. A great percentage was less likely to develop pulmonary edema. One of the most remarkable facts was that none needed artificial breathing apparatus. This single study provided some fascinating truths about prayer: Prayer, when used as an additional method of healing, can be far more powerful than medication.

There is no distance requirement for prayer to work. The scientific aspect of mind is being proven. Mind doesn't travel like radio waves that dissipate after so many miles. A prayer works whether the person is in the same room or thousands of miles away.

Had this study been to try out the effectiveness of a new drug, the entire media would have carried the story. Instead, a small article appeared in a San Francisco newspaper stating, "Wasn't this an interesting experiment?"

Modern medical cures are not only being helped along by prayer. Family physicians will continue to dispense pills, serums and ointments. However, in these modern times we have many choices of alternative treatments.

~ Osteopaths and chiropractors manipulate bones and muscles.

~ Acupuncturists and masseuses release blocked energy flow.

~ Ministers, practitioners and counselors work on physical challenges using the power of the mind.

~ Herbologists dispense powders, teas and poultices.

The astounding part is most of these modalities get good results. As ancient Taoist philosopher, Lao Tsu said, "When the student is ready, the teacher appears." How can so many different methods be effective? Because healing is done in the realm of mind, as proven time and time again by the mysterious placebo.

**You Are Your Own Placebo**

Placebo comes from the Latin word, "I shall please." Over the years these little non-pharmaceutical pills have seemed to work wonders.

In one study, doctors administered placebos to half of their patients who had bleeding ulcers. They were told this new "wonder drug" would eliminate all their ailments. Over 70% of their medical problems disappeared. The other half was told that the placebo was just an experimental drug with unknown results. Only 25% of them improved.

Half of a group of post-operative patients were

given morphine to ease their pain. 50% of them felt relief. The other half was given a placebo, and 40% of them reported they felt no pain. In yet another study, drug addicts found placebo injections to be equally as effective as methadone.

Nowadays, researchers use saline injections or sugar pills as placebos. But non-medicinal cure-alls have a long history. In the past, people used animal dung, lizard blood or eye of newt. Snake oil salesmen traveled the country selling their magic wares. How did mysterious healing take place when there was no medical basis for the healing? We only know it seemed to be the faith of the person using the placebo. People who have a great deal of confidence in their physician will respond best to medical treatment. People will go to a doctor whose name they can't pronounce, receive a prescription written in writing they can't read and take the pill for an ailment they don't understand. This is faith healing. It is not so much the pill that heals, but the belief of the individual receiving the cure. Faith healing is not a method trusted by the mainstream population. Medicine is chemical intelligence and we are in physical bodies that do respond. Yet if a placebo is not faith healing, what else can it be called?

While Norman Cousins studied with Dr. Albert Schweitzer in Africa, they went out into the jungle to see a witch doctor in action. They observed as natives came to the witch doctor that he sent some home with a bag of roots, herbs and seeds, while he simply repeated some incantations and wave his hands over others. After Cousins watched the scene for a while, he asked Schweitzer what was going on.

"The first group of people had commonplace symptoms. The witch doctor knew no matter what kind of mixture he put in the bag, the ailment would go away." The second group was going through the African style of psychotherapy. Cousins had trouble believing the people could be healed by a witch doctor. Schweitzer remarked, "That witch doctor knows what all good doctors have known since the days of Hippocrates. He knows within each person is an inner doctor and the physician's best work comes when he can help the patient release that inner power to do the work. "

The truth of our nature is one of perfect health. We have an innate intelligence within every cell of our being. Ernest Holmes states, "Healing is not just a process, but a revelation of the perfect being. For the process, if there is one, it is the time and the thought it takes to arrive at the correct understanding of one's perfect state." In my role as a minister, I often watch healing unfold as soon as my clients ask me to pray. Once I tell them, "Everything is going to be all right," they believe the condition will disappear, and so the process of healing begins. As we begin to realize we have the power within us, we can get excited about the unlimited possibilities of being immersed in a wave of healing in our body as well as our affairs.

## Kahunas of Healing

Max Freedom Long was a researcher into the Hawaiian language. In his work on the Huna energies, he said, "When the Kahunas dealt with healing, the first thing they did was to get the mind and the consciousness clean." All the parasitic emotions such as guilt, fear and resentment were to be removed. They went through a ceremony of forgiveness. The Huna philosophy believes healing takes place when there's a restoration of the energy flow. When negative emotions are held for any length of time, the flow is blocked and tension results. The generic term for illness in Hawaiian is ma'i, which means, "a state of tension or restriction."

Just as there are three aspects of surfing, one must be physically prepared, mentally ready and willing to paddle out into the power energy of the surf. Hawaiian healers, the Kahunas use a combination of therapies in their practice, beginning with the physical. They may start with the reopening of the energy pathways through massage and physical exercise. The healers also work in the realm of the client's mind by leading him through a process, which teaches him to take charge of his own thinking. The Kahunas believe Divine Healing is the most important of the three strategies. Serge Kahili King, in Kahuna Healing, says, "The most direct healing of body, mind and circumstance comes through consciously involving the God-Self in your daily life." Do not let your feelings control your life. You need to get yourself out of the way of Spirit's healing power. You are the only thing impeding its flow.

Occasionally, people believe they've earned the right to feel bad. I've watched some defend their depression as if it were an ally instead of an enemy. ("I'm depressed because my relationship just broke up." "My unemployment has really put me into a funk.") These kinds of people just know the letter from the IRS contains a tax due notice, not a refund. When the phone rings, they're sure it's going to be catastrophic news about a friend. There are those who even worry about being happy because they know good feelings can't last.

When our minds are in discord, it's difficult to feel harmony. When we've got our mind concentrated on problems, it's tough to hear God, and healing is next to impossible. The mind cannot think two contrasting thoughts at once, nor can the body feel two opposite emotions. How can you be at peace in the same moment you feel anger? And how can you expect good when you are thinking negative thoughts? The waves do not discriminate, nor does the life force moving through this world. If you are afraid, your mind will inhibit your body's movement, making it nearly impossible to put together a sequence of maneuvers across the face of the wave. As such, resentment, anger, bitterness put a lump in your body, impeding your joyous ride through life.

What is it you worry about? How much does this help you? Do you remember what you were worrying about last year? Worrying never solves problems. Fear doesn't heal anything. Guilt doesn't stop us from repeating negative patterns. And resentment doesn't affect anyone but the resenter. These are parasitic emotions keeping the healing energy away. You can always transcend human conditions, but your mind needs to be focused on your intended results. When you are very clear about what you want to accomplish, healing can take place instantly.

When I'm sitting out in the water, looking at the expansive ocean, my mind fully focused on enjoying the swells at hand, the problems of life are left behind me on the land. Just as the natural metamorphoses of the calm summer season quiet the exciting winter by filling the holes of the reefs with sand, so nature knows how to fill and smooth the rough places of our being.

**Restoration to Wholeness**

My former church in Ventura was housed in a building, which was designated as a historical landmark. Designed by the famous Stacey Judd, it was unique Mayan architecture. He had gone down to the Yucatan Peninsula on a Carnegie Grant, and assisted with the excavation of the Mayan Ruins. He returned with the desire to construct a building that would incorporate Mayan structures.

Our building had a huge Mayan tower, reaching to the heavens. There was an inverted, seven-step ceiling, each step representing one day of creation. The thick walls were covered in mystical symbolism. Downstairs was a basement with numerous rooms, one of which housed our junior church.

I was preparing to walk out for the first service. Each Sunday, our keyboardist gave me my music cue exactly on the hour. Her eyes were fixed on the clock. As I was about to make my entrance, a teen-aged boy approached me and said, "Our teacher just tumbled down the stairs. She doesn't look very good."

Meanwhile, the congregation was waiting for me to step onto the stage. I had a quick decision to make. Would I make my entrance on time or take care of my teacher? My choice was clear. I rushed downstairs and there was Marcella, sprawled out on the floor. Her face was bruised from bouncing off the cement walls. Her left wrist was hanging limp, obviously broken.

She knew exactly what she wanted to happen. Her belief in the power of prayer was immensely strong. "Christian," she said, "do your prayer work on me." All the kids were standing by, watching us. They wanted to see their spiritual leader prove his stuff and their beloved teacher to show them how healing really works.

I sat there praying quietly for several minutes. Then Marcella, all the children and I prayed together. After awhile, feeling my work was done, I returned to the sanctuary. The service would be delayed only ten minutes—or so I thought.

An amazing phenomenon had occurred. While I was doing my healing work downstairs, the reliable clock in the sanctuary had actually stopped running. I knew this because after the service, Anna, who had been sitting in the front row, wearing a watch and eyeing the clock, told me so. My keyboardist, waiting for the hour to strike, kept playing the pre-service music. Just as I walked up the last stair, the clock struck nine, the music cue was played, and the service went on as planned and on time.

Immediately after the service, Marcella went to the doctor. The x-rays showed indeed there had been a break. However, they also indicated the bone had already gone back together —on its own.

It's important not to get caught up in what the outside world says is fact. Nothing has the last say in our world, unless we give up our power. Doctors have given death sentences to people who later outlived them. People run who were told they would never walk again. Spirit is far greater than any physical fact, if you are willing to snap your leash of attachment to be immersed in God's wave of healing.

Granted, we sometimes find ourselves in precarious situations. We're still working on becoming. Our whole life is about becoming and revealing our true, spiritual nature. We need to keep open to the Divine Presence that is seeking to birth itself in our life. To do this we often have to remove ourselves from difficult situations. At times, the most spiritual thing we can do is to stop reading books, turn off the TV, take a hiatus from classes, and transport our body and mind elsewhere for a while. The location can be near or far. However, it must be a place that brings our awareness into alignment with its authentic higher self, the part of us that knows and is willing to connect with our spiritual truth. It's the true self, seeking to know itself—the self who is willing to look out upon the horizon of possibilities, as opposed to staying focused on the land locked consciousness.

# Five

# No Problem

*There was no way we could climb
fast. The terrain of the mountain
and the high altitude, forced us
to slow down. As we moved slower
and slower, our hearts beat faster and faster.
The trek became more a matter
of surviving than conquering.
When we saw the first ancient archway
of the gates to the monastery,
the exhilaration was intense
and exciting. We stood
on the pinnacle, thousands of feet
above the valley, now obscured by the clouds
that roll in each afternoon. It looked as if
we were in the middle of a milky ocean.
Reverence for this spectacular site filled our
beings. I knew I was experiencing
one of those perfect waves.*

# Chapter 5

# NO PROBLEM

### No Problem

One travels the planet looking for the perfect wave to drop in on—steep, thrilling, treacherously powerful, with mean, deep tubes. God and the day-to-day check permitting, one day you find yourself in the perfect place to say "good morning" to the "beast" as it thunderously awakes upon the outer reefs. Why do we do this? For the same reason as our forefathers—it's fun!

The dauntless dozen from Seaside Church was poised for an exotic adventure. We were finally embarking on the exciting journey we had planned for so long. Tingling with anticipation, I was reminded of those times I'd set out in search of the perfect wave. In those quests, I've found it's easy to get caught up in the belief the wave was going to look a certain way, be found in a certain place and the ride was going to follow a certain dynamic course. Part of nature's most dazzling beauty would certainly include speed (with its exhilaration). Yet, the perfect waves of life don't always include speed, just as one has waiting periods or holding time for the window of opportunity to present itself. Catching the spirit in such waves sometimes means slowing down, putting aside preconceived ideas of where and how it will be found, and what it will look like. This was one of the lessons brought home to my Western heart while on our exciting journey into an Eastern culture—lessons learned high atop a mountain, far from any ocean waves.

Just as many go to the North Shore of Oahu, the Mecca of big, perfect waves, for the winter season, so many head for the Himalayas a spiritual Mecca upon this planet. Our first set of lessons emerged quickly. Before we boarded the plane to Nepal, Joel complained about his seat location. "Who wants to sit in the middle of the row?" he grumbled.

Being the leader of the group, I felt it my duty to calm him down. "Don't worry, once we take off, you can switch with somebody else," I assured him.

Once the plane lifted gently off the runway at LAX, everyone settled in for the lengthy flight. Soon the midday meal was served. "Chicken or beef?" the flight attendant asked me.

"I ordered vegetarian," I answered.

"Sorry, sir. There's no record of any special order," she replied.

Anger welled up in me at not getting my way. "Why can't the airlines get things right? Don't they know how important my nutritional program is?" I muttered.

Twenty hours later, walking through Katmandu for the first time, I realized just how insignificant our problems really were.

Hundreds of people slept out on the streets, or lived their lives for years in handmade dwellings of cardboard placed precariously on the roadsides. They had no other place to go. There were some who were starving to death almost before our eyes. Seeing such poverty drastically changes one's perspective. When survival is at stake, seat assignments, in-flight meals and other petty grievances no longer seem critical.

Thinking back to my trek through the Himalayas

always fills me with great reverence. I didn't have any Divine revelations. The universe didn't open up and pour forth all its answers for me. I didn't even go back to past life experiences and find profound understanding of my reason for being. Yet I did learn many lasting lessons—and began to see life in an entirely different way. The wave didn't look like I thought it would. Yet the experience was more awesome than I had expected.

As I walked through the countryside, I realized I hadn't seen a car, motorcycle, or even one piece of machinery. Since life moves at such a slow pace, you have to slow down. After a few days of walking from place to place instead of driving, my body felt stronger. My mind became clearer and the beauty surrounding me seemed more vivid.

The Sherpas came down from the hillsides to greet us with a smile and a "Namaste." You could feel their sincerity. After all, they didn't have to check their day planner to schedule a visit with you. They were genuinely overjoyed to be with you. We couldn't communicate verbally, but our bonding at the heart level was evident. Our entire group felt that connection later as we joined together with our guides, dancing to the rhythm of their primitive drums and hand made flutes. The dance was not a celebration of any specific event, but one of sheer, spontaneous joy.

Arnold Toynbee said, "The Himalayas have a message to give (modern) man...that message is one of hope. It is still possible for man to regain his original concord with nature, which will bring him salvation from his present man-made plight."

We walked up there and felt a tremendous sense of community. The Nepalese work with each other in such harmony. While cocooning is popular in our society, isolation from other people is not possible there, if survival is the goal. Staying at home, watching the latest movies on your VCR or talking on the Internet allows for survival in our culture, but over there people have to labor together in order to survive. One grows the grain and the other raises the Yak. This sharing is what makes their society work.

The morning after our arrival in Bangkok, Thailand, I woke up early and went outside. A Buddhist monk came walking towards me. His head was shaved, he wore a chiffon robe and was barefoot. Down the street he moved with his bowl, seeking offerings. People kneeled before him and prayed—not to worship him, but to symbolically surrender to the spirit he represented. Then, as he looked away, they would put their meager offerings into his bowl.

The streets of Bangkok are filled with color and sound. Hundreds of kiosks overflowing with souvenir items crowd the sidewalks. Tuk-tuks, small motor scooters, serve as taxis, doing their best not to hit pedestrians who walk in the middle of the street. People sell their chickens, roots, vegetables, fish and frogs. Strange odors make your head spin, eyes water and stomach turn as they permeate the thick, warm air.

A man touched me on my shoulder. Immediately, I thrust my hands into my pockets and stepped back. I realized I brought my Western suspicion of strangers with me to those crowded Eastern streets. "What does he want from me?" I thought. What he wanted was an opportunity to sit with me over a cup of tea. He knew I was American and he had been planning a trip to the states. All he really wanted was to talk. But my Western time clock was still running, I glanced at my watch and said, "Sorry, I have to be out of here in five minutes."

After I returned from the trek through the mountains, I seized every possible opportunity to connect with the locals. I found myself stopping in the streets of Katmandu to feed the hungry and pray with the poor and the dying. It's amazing how life can shape us to the perfect design if we give it a little time.

**You Did What**

Being over there forced me to slow down. We waited for our charter plane to the backcountry of the Himalayas. Over here charter planes wait for their passengers and for the designated time of departure, then they take off. In that part of the world, however, they don't follow the same rules. This is neither right nor wrong, just a different way of living. We were told to arrive at the airport by 7:00 a.m. and also warned the plane might not leave on time; in fact, if we took off by 9:00 a.m. it would be unusual.

An hour passed, the clouds and fog began to lift. At 10:00 a.m., we still waited. "What's going on?" I asked the clerk.

"Oh, nothing serious. It's just that we gave your plane to some other passengers this morning."

Who knew where our Everest Air flight was or when the next one would be free? We were loud in vocalizing our Western discontent. At noon the airlines canceled future flights due to bad weather.

Dark clouds rolled into the area. The winds kicked up and the sky was filled with birds which historically fly before a storm. Finally our plane arrived. Unfortunately, our pilot took one look at the stormy skies and decided to go home. He said the weather wasn't good enough for us to land on the mountain.

Addressing the manager, I suggested what any busy American would, "Why don't you call someone on the mountain and see if it's possible for us to land?"

"Sir," he replied politely, "you don't understand. There's only a dirt runway and no tower. I can't call. They don't have a phone up there!"

"Then let's take off and find a hole through the clouds," I reasoned.

He called another pilot, who agreed to fly the plane. By now the storms had really moved in. We slipped into the tight, twelve-seater plane and took off. A few moments later, the aircraft started bouncing us all over the skies like a steel ball in a pinball machine. We dropped hundreds of feet at a time and visibility was zero. We all hoped there were no mountain peaks at our altitude. Suddenly, we climbed above the storm.

It felt as if we were dancing on the cloud tops. The majestic, snow-covered peaks of the Mt. Everest range came into view. Unfortunately, the air to ground visibility was so bad it would have been impossible to land safely. So the pilot turned the little plane around and we went back.

Surprisingly, there wasn't a tremendous sense of disappointment in our group. We were just glad we didn't die attempting a dangerous landing. And we did catch a bird's eye glimpse of many snow-capped peaks of the legendary Himalayas—experiencing a shared feeling of intense awe. I recognized it as the same sense I've had when "the veil parts" during meditation. For a few brief moments, I am totally connected with Spirit and I just

know.  We saw the mountains and knew there was something more in store for us, knew we would go back and
enjoy their magnificence.  Our attitude was not "what a
horrible experience."  Instead, we knew "things happen
for the best."  The Nepalese have a saying, "Que
garne...oh well!"  We knew this was a perfect moment, just
not the way we had planned.

That night in Katmandu, the natives held an
incredible Hindu celebration on the rooftops of the city.
Fireworks filled the sky.  Children danced in the streets
and knocked on doors, it was their form of trick or treat.
Had we not been forced to come back to the city, we would
have missed this exciting expression of their culture.

During the celebration we took part in our own
rooftop ceremony of letting go.  We visualized some part in
our lives we thought were holding us back.  As if there
were a string binding these things to us, we took a large
knife placed on hand woven silk scarves and mentally cut
the ties and let them go into the winds.  Then we visualized
those gifts we wished to receive and poured them into a
Tibetan Singing Bowl placed before us.

## Thank You, God

The next day we flew through blue skies and
smooth air to the mountaintop runway.  Once we saw the
landing strip, we were glad the pilot had turned around the
day before.  The dirt runway was no longer than a football
field.  It was laid out on an incline, because at the end of
the hundred yards was a cliff going straight down!

We got off the plane and were ready to conquer the
mountain peak where we would reach the holy monastery
of Chiwang Gompa, the Monastery of the Clouds.  Our

hurry-up, microwave minds thought, "Let's do it now!"

There was no way we could climb fast. The terrain of the mountain and the high altitude, forced us to slow down. As we moved slower and slower, our hearts beat faster and faster. The trek became more a matter of surviving than conquering. When we saw the first ancient archway of the gates to the monastery, the exhilaration was intense and exciting. We stood on the pinnacle, thousands of feet above the valley, now obscured by the clouds that roll in each afternoon. It looked as if we were in the middle of a milky ocean. Reverence for this spectacular site filled our beings. I knew I was experiencing one of those perfect waves.

We could have complained about how tough the trekking became. Had we done this, our hearts would not have been open to receive the gift of the scenery, the magical moment or the kindness of the lamas. By the laws of attraction and repulsion, we would have repelled the gift we were offered and now accepted.

Our commercials tell us in order to attract who and what we want in our lives, we need to use the right cologne, after-shave and soap. "Change your mouthwash, change your life," they say. While effective advertising, such messages are at best incomplete. In the Himalayas I once again realized we are always either attracting or repelling. Like magnets, we attract into our lives those experiences that we are ready to receive. When you are willing to be in concord and harmony with your environment, you receive the gifts life has to offer. If you don't like what's coming into your world, stop feeding it and it will go away.

Do you have an unwanted houseguest who has overstayed his welcome?

Empty your refrigerator. With nothing to eat, your guest will soon depart—hungry but gone.

Think of metal filings stuck to a magnet. Remove the magnetic field and the filings fall to the ground.

Weeds will not thrive in your garden if they are deprived of moisture. Keep water from them and they will die.

Stop feeding the weeds of negativity in your life and they will also die. The reverse is also just as true. "The bread you cast upon the water comes back to you," says the Bible. "As you sow, so shall you reap." This is the law. Instead of sowing the seeds of discontent about our situation, we accepted the delay as Spirit's way of telling us to slow down, be patient and wait.

Sitting high atop the awesome mountain peak, we realized the wait was worth it. We also became aware the trek was not about conquering the mountain. It was about being part of the surroundings. Each day nature gave us more and more beautiful gifts because we became attuned to the energy. In surfing, you can ride when you feel the energy.

As we hiked through lush forests the next day, we noticed the gifts. Green moss hung over the many streams we crossed. Multi-colored flowers grew on the riverbanks. Waterfalls cascaded down hillsides. We picked and ate wild raspberries, their flavor exploding in our mouths. Ingesting a part of the unspoiled environment helped us all to honor where we were and to be fully present in the wave of God's perfect moment.

### At One

One of the Sherpa guides began to play his harmonica. Caught up in the rhythm of the music, I started clapping. Before I realized what was happening, I dropped my daypack and started dancing, swinging around close to this beautiful waterfall. With no thought of who was watching, the rest of my group opened up and allowed the Spirit to move through them in joy.

The Sherpas seemed less like spectators than part of the environment. We knew they were not judging us, but were simply being there to share and smile. As the minutes passed, we also felt as if we belonged there—trees, water, rocks, Sherpas, trekkers.

I can remember watching a film on the Discovery Channel. There were small iron shavings in a tray. One of the participants standing near made a tinkling sound by striking a triangle. The shavings moved into the form of a snowflake. Another tone was sounded and the flakes went into the shape of a star. The metal particles responded to the sounds around them by changing their normal shapes to what looked more like the surrounding environment. We, the Western dancers on the mountain, followed suit.

In the evening after dinner our porters would build a campfire. The music started again, but this time the harmonicas were accompanied by drums. Between the beating of the drums, clapping and chanting, there seemed to be a primeval energy stirring. We were under a canopy of bright stars, with a sliver of a moon in the sky. There was no way I could sit still. Once again tossing aside my Western self-conscious nature, I'd find myself hopping around, leaping over the flames of the campfire and letting out my own primeval spirit. We weren't trying to force a bonding experience as might happen in our own country. We were just being in the experience, at one with the perfect wave.

Awaking the next morning, muscles stiff but feeling refreshed from a deep, restful sleep, we hiked up another mountainside. After stopping for lunch, we walked across a long, rope bridge, suspended high over powerfully roaring rapids. Then our head Sherpa told us we were about to climb what he called, "a gradual up." In English this means, "straight up!" The first hour went by and my legs burned from the strain. Another hour passed and we began slipping in the soft mud. Awhile later, the group separated as some went ahead and others lagged behind. We continued up the mountain. My legs continued to burn and my lungs were oxygen deprived from the altitude. One man in our group had to lie down every few minutes to catch his breath and get his irregular heartbeat back into rhythm.

The Sherpas, who had already arrived at the top, came back to us on the trail. Born high in the mountains, their hearts and lungs were used to the altitude and the physical exertion. They carried tea, biscuits and popcorn with them, tokens of their affection and caring. When we finally got to the camp, the rest of the guides were overjoyed to see us. It didn't matter some of us took longer to get there, as long as we arrived safely. We had all conquered the mountain together, at least to this height.

Our sleeping arrangements left much to be desired: We were still on a steep incline, so our guides had to carve a large niche out of the hillside bushes. We slept in what seemed almost a vertical position, tied to the tree stumps at 12,000 feet. By early evening ice covered the ground. The heavens looked like a giant colander where the stars were the light on the other side of the bowl. One could see the satellites traveling on their course as if on a highway.

The next morning we moved higher. We knew some

of the group would not make this part of the trek, but it didn't matter. By then we knew if any one of us could make it to the top, it was for all of us, now a unified body. Under still sparkling stars, the Sherpas awakened us at 4:00 a.m. At 5:00 a.m. we looked down upon the sun rising over glaciered peaks and into brilliant, pink skies. What a magnificent sight! The hills were covered with ice. We ascended up to over 14,000 feet, having to stop every hundred yards to keep our heads from spinning. Then the stops became more frequent, but we kept going.

By the time we got to the top, the view was incredible. Mt. Everest was in full view and we were looking down at airplanes flying and eagles soaring. There was no way to deny Spirit was right there in our midst. I carried personal prayers from my congregation in my pocket. I had promised them I would find the perfect spot in the Himalayas to do my prayer work. Piles of ceremonial stones lay on the ground where others had prayed before me. On that very spot, I fulfilled my promise and lifted a prayer flag to the wind to carry my thoughts.

**Their Way**

Being in Nepal and Thailand made me contemplate how we Westerners live in a strange, mental world, where we've lost touch with our physical senses. When I want to know what the weather is like at home, I don't walk outside to see for myself, I turn on the TV Weather Channel. On the other hand, in the Himalayas, I tasted wild spearmint and thought, "This is just like chewing gum." And my ears waited for the hum of traffic to break the silence.

We have created elaborate techniques in child psychology. Yet, often the solution to the problem is just to give the kids more smiles and hugs. Fritz Perls said, "Real psychotherapy is losing one's mind and finding our senses." Trekking through the Himalayas makes your mind more receptive to what seem to be unconventional customs and lifestyles.

Traveling in the East, things don't fit into our Western consciousness. With camels tied to its entrance, one Sheraton Hotel in India has snake charmers in front, sitting with their dancing cobras. In the lobby the money-changing booth stands next to the astrology booth. On the side of the roads, dancing bears entertain passersby. Close to town, wild animals roam free. Elephants walk through the streets, carrying boxes and bags; and taxi and bus drivers definitely don't follow any Western vehicular laws.

When we arrived, a national strike had just begun. Buses were parked in the middle of the road as transportation was shut down and armed national guardsmen walked the streets. From our perspective, the poverty, sickness and sanitation appeared horrible. It made me realize our challenges back home were not insurmountable. As I walked through the Himalayas looking for Shangri-La, I knew where it was—right here at home. We have the closest thing to perfection.

We can create our own Shangri-La. The task begins with us. I pray the modern world does not desecrate the Himalayas in the name of progress. Those peaks continue to be a spiritual Mecca. Whether one makes it there in form or in consciousness, it is a spiritual place that heightens one's awareness and slows one down.

We have mastered the physical world. Some have scaled every peak in the Himalayas. We've set out to conquer the physical world and have forgotten ourselves.

~ "Know thyself"...Shakespeare

~ "To conquer oneself is the first and greatest victory"...Plato

~ "The best battle to win is with oneself"...Socrates

     You can search the globe for the perfect wave, climb Mt. Shasta or Mt. Everest, visit the sacred temples of the world or bathe in the waters of Lourdes, but unless you realize the answer lies within you, it doesn't matter where you go. When you return, the bliss will leave you quickly. Begin, instead, to search within and you will discover that Shangri-La—that perfect wave of life— is right where you are. All you need do is slow down and open up to accepting the gifts surrounding you and you will experience the definitive ride of your life.

# Six

# The Lull Between Waves

*When I'm out surfing and my mind
is filled with fear that the next wave
is going to come crashing down in
front of me, spinning me around
like a crow in a tornado,
it's impossible to be present in
the moment where Spirit speaks.
Even in wild times there are gaps
or lulls between the action,
allowing you to catch your breath
and restore your perspective.*

# Chapter 6

# THE LULL BETWEEN WAVES

## Choose Your Own Distraction

The opportunity to leave all the noise, confusion and challenges behind is one of the great joys of jumping in the water and paddling out. Facing an open ocean where the waves move in, my terrestrial problems remain back on land. I am immersed in the moment and without distractions.

Modern day people work hard; there are meetings, classes, families to care for, chores to finish and goals to achieve. In the rush of attempting to get somewhere, we often forget one of the most important aspects of a balanced life—rest. Even God rested on the seventh day.

We're fortunate we live in a society that honors time off from work. Government offices are closed on weekends, and Congress has even declared several three-day holidays throughout the year. Yet, our society is not moving towards more rest, but away from it. Years ago, you couldn't find a store open on Sundays, banks closed on Friday afternoons and reopened Monday morning, all school years were finished by June. Now, we have banks open on Saturdays, weekend and holiday sales at retail stores and many year-round schools. The technology age is supposed to give us more leisure time, yet we seem to be working more and enjoying life less.

Along with an increased activity schedule, we're bombarded with noise and pictures. A quiet beach walk is no longer possible with the boom boxes playing and radios blasting from passing cars, advertisers projecting their images into our minds every where we turn.

On a recent ski trip, my friend and I were about to tackle a white, powdery slope. We stood on top of the steep hill, drinking in the beauty of the mountain and the quiet of nature. My eyes had been closed for just a moment when I heard an unfamiliar sound, almost like a bass drum thumping. The sound turned into a noise that grew louder each second. I turned around and up from behind me roared two teen-aged boys on snowmobiles, stereos turned up to maximum volume. "Even at 10,000 feet," I thought, "it's hard to get away from noise pollution."

There's no such thing as waiting for anything in peace and quiet anymore. Companies play music over the phone while you're waiting for the party you called. Department stores play music over the loud speakers. Post offices flash news across a screen and car rental agencies show you videos of tourist spots in the city you're visiting.

Many of us seem unable to go without visual or auditory stimuli. School kids study while listening to loud music and watching videos at the same time. How often do people sit at home in the stillness, without the radio or TV turned on, if only for noise value.

Bill, my long-time friend, moved his family from Malibu to a Mid-western farm. After just three months, they returned to California. "Why did you come back so quickly?" I asked him.

"Christian, I'll tell you the truth," he answered candidly, "We just couldn't stand the silence."

Can you stand the silence? Can you do without reading a newspaper for a few days? Can you keep the TV and CD players turned off? For your general well-being and in order to get more in touch with a higher power, you have to quiet down. Try this for just one week and notice how much clearer your thoughts become.

Most people think of surfing as an action sport. It's true, you do have to paddle out, a sort of jogging with the arms, over the breaking waves; and once you catch a wave, all your energy is directed towards getting the most out of it. But between rides there is "the lull"— the still, waiting time before the next set of waves comes in. The lull is a wonderful meditation time. Paddling out, you're with friends, a part of the crew. But once you get to the lineup and begin your wait, you're alone with your thoughts, hopes and fears. I've made life-changing decisions while waiting for the next wave. At times, I've even crossed over into the spiritual realm, the space one seldom experiences but yearns to know.

**Out of the Darkness**

In 1982, accompanied by my childhood friend, Tony, I took a trip to Egypt and visited the Great Pyramids, including the Pyramid of Cheops. Though the hot sun was baking the desert floor, when I stepped through a hole in the wall of the structure, the air became cool and damp. There was hardly any light, and as I began to move through the narrow passage my eyes adjusted to the semi-darkness. The only light came from a string of tiny bulbs hanging from the walls. Arriving at the passage to the king's chambers, I paused, speculating on what I'd find inside, when all the lights went out. I stood there, wondering what had happened.

In a few moments, I noticed candles coming down from the upper passage. The guard was escorting the tourists out; but I decided to stay. Suddenly I was alone in the dark chamber. I took out my flashlight and pointed it up the passage. My head hit against the low ceiling and my back rubbed the walls. A story about Napoleon, who was said to have gone crazy after having slept in the pyramids, came to mind. Hopefully, this wasn't what was in store for me.

I came out into a chamber of pure blackness— alone, except for a sarcophagus, the king's tomb. I lay down in the royal coffin and my mind started to entertain the worst. I envisioned snakes and scorpions coming to get me, or worse, ghostly spirits. Yet, once I got beyond all these fears, another realm appeared, a place of utter calm.

As if in a deep sleep, my mind wandered. I lost all track of time. But when the lights came back on and I heard the guard coming towards me, I jumped out of the sarcophagus, my dream state gone. I knew I had experienced something very profound, but in the light of day only the feeling remained. Something in me had shifted. It's all right to enter the quiet lull.

Throughout the ages great thinkers have left behind the conflicts of this world to touch a higher spiritual state. When their ideas were brought back to fertile soil, they made a huge difference in the world. Krishna, Buddha, Zarathustra and many others espoused ideas that have lasted throughout the centuries.

## A Patient Apprentice

Eastern literature is filled with sword masters and apprentice stories all following similar patterns. In order to learn from a great sword master, a young man decides to apprentice himself to a guru. First, he gives up his material possessions; then begins his long journey to the master's house. Along the way he encounters many challenges, including having to make his way through a dangerous, enchanted forest.

Upon finally reaching the master's house, our apprentice knocks on the master's door. The master looks out the window, sees the young man and says, "Go away!" But the visitor, not knowing he wants to learn patience, sits down instead of leaving. He sits waiting outside the master's door for an extended period of time.

One day, the master comes out holding a piece of bamboo and touches the apprentice's shoulder, startling him. "Now," he says, "this is your first lesson in alertness." Then the master asks him to do some menial chores around the house, just like the Karate Kid of movie fame. Over several months, the apprentice develops his own mastery.

Our society has few such stories. How many of us would sit outside a master's house for an hour, let alone a month? We stand in front of a microwave, waiting 8 minutes instead of an hour for a potato to bake, and yell, "Hurry up!" Evidence of our impatience also lies in the titles in the bookstores:

~ Fitness in just 12 minutes a week
~ The One-Minute Manger
~ Seven days to Perfect Health

Mastery takes time. (Sorry to reconfirm this notion, but if didn't I would have figured a way around it by now.) Life is about the journey, not the destination. Living is a continual process of becoming. We need to sit back, take a look at our personal world and say, "Although there may be things I want to do, my life is generally going well."

Musicians play a set and take a break. Baseball games have a seventh inning stretch. Even God was said to have rested on the seventh day. The McDonald's jingle says it best. "You deserve a break today." Don't get so caught up in having "to do" that you miss out on the beauty of the world around you and the light within you. Know the lull is an integral part of the ride and to be enjoyed, not rushed through.

A few weeks ago, my wife and I went up into the mountains. Building a fire, I watched the logs explode with the lights, and was filled with a sense of awe at how the wood captured the energy of the sun. We listened to the soft rain on the roof of the condo. Rain doesn't need any kind of mental analysis or interpretation. Rain is just magical.

Go watch a tomato "tomatoing". When was the last time you looked closely at a fire, a goldfish or a precious plant?

Quantum physicists tell us there is more going on in the spaces between atoms than in the atoms themselves. Your challenges will be resolved faster if you allow space in your life. Take a break. Get in touch with the universal intelligence within you that always knows the answer.

## Don't be Late

One summer I was asked to officiate at a wedding, which was to be held at a beautiful church. My car's clock told me the wedding would begin in five minutes. I thought, "If I make every green light, find the perfect parking spot (remedial metaphysics), grab my robe, run across the parking lot and streak across the lawn, I'll be there exactly on time." Then I had another thought, "Christian, why do you stress yourself out like this? Why do you give Spirit so many barriers." Still, I hurried.

The last light was green and the parking lot appeared in my vision. I turned the last corner and my heart sank. The street leading to the church was under construction—closed! There was absolutely no way to get where I wanted to go using my plan on how to get there on time.

Often you set goals in life and formulate a plan to get there. Then, all of a sudden, the road is blocked. Life doesn't turn out quite like you thought it would. Your first instinct is to try harder. This is the exact time you need to take a break, get quiet and let Spirit handle the situation.

I looked at the "Road Closed" sign and said, "Okay, God, I've blown it here. What can I do? Get me out of this situation. Beam me up, Buddha." I parked the car, walked quickly down the street to the parking lot and across the football field. As I opened the door, the groom greeted me and said, "I'm glad you're a little late, Christian. My bride was delayed and just arrived."

Slow down and find your inner peace. I looked at my leisure time: surfing, skiing, flying, football, tennis and scuba diving, all action-packed activities. Now, I've taken up Yoga to slow down both my body and my mind. I can barely touch my knees without bending them, reaching down to my ankles is next to impossible, and the ground is only a dream. At first I had to force myself to stop pushing so hard to touch the ground. If only I could appreciate the moment and the process, the ground would one day find its way up to my fingertips. For me, most difficult was moving more slowly than I ever moved before and stopping the chatter of my brain. However, I take heart in noticing

I'm not the only one with this challenge. Lots of us trip over ourselves because we're in such a hurry.

One morning as my neighbor and I left the house at the same time, I noticed she was carrying her daily supply of luggage. We exchanged "good morning" waves and she turned to lock her front door, then began to pick up her bags: first her purse, then her briefcase and her lunch bag, next her gym bag—and finally, the trash bag. Obviously, she was trying to handle everything in one trip. Her arms overloaded, she stepped towards her car. All of a sudden her scream pierced the early morning quiet. I looked over to see she had walked into one of those giant spider webs often stretched, like an insect tightrope, high-wired across a sidewalk. All the bags went flying in different directions. Pawing at her face and hair, she pranced a high-stepping jig, looking like a stork in heat. I'm sure in her mind the spider was lobster-sized with poisonous fangs, ready to spring. Dashing to the front door, she frantically fumbled with the key and broke it in half. My final glimpse was of her racing out to the backyard. I think I heard the sound of the hose washing her down. In spite of trying to save precious minutes by carrying everything at once, she left the house almost an hour later—after a second shower and a fresh change of clothes. Instead of saving time, she arrived at the office late.

W. C. Fields said, "If at first you don't succeed, try, try again, then quit. There's no need making a damn fool out of yourself." If there's a challenge in our lives, we tend to think trying harder will fix it faster. The contrary is true. If we can just take a break from worry, doubt and anxiety, Universal Intelligence will find the solution. You and I can either put forth great effort, hurry, push and muscle our way through life, or slow down and let Spirit do the work.

## God, the Mechanic

After church one stormy, wintry day, I headed up towards Mammoth Mountain, in Northern California. There was a board meeting that day, so my departure was delayed until late afternoon. By the time my wife and I pulled into the Mojave Desert, it was nearing eleven o'clock. The moonless sky was pitch black and the road deserted. Suddenly the car began to make a loud, knocking sound. "Christian," my wife volunteered, her voice shaky, "I don't like how the car sounds."

"So turn on the radio," I replied. We both hoped the sound would disappear on its own, for I possess no mechanical ability whatsoever. The noise only got louder, until, in a burst of smoke, the engine blew up.

There we were, just the two of us, in the middle of the Mojave Desert, rain pouring down with neither of us knowing anything about car engines. But I tried—I opened the hood, hoping to see something obvious. As the flashlight lit up the engine area, I noticed the spark plug wires were not attached, but hanging loosely. I knew enough about motors to know this was not a good sign, but not enough to know what to do. Someone had to go for help. My mind began trying to come up with a solution.

"Leave my wife in the car and go for help? Leave her alone? We may never see each other again...Send her for help and stay with car? Possibly the same result...Get out on the road and hitchhike together?" My mind fought that idea. "Sure," it countered, "I can envision the scene now. A trucker picks us up, tells me to get out and drives off with my wife. Then what?" I knew I had to quiet my mind's chatter of fear and "what ifs" and enter into a more peaceful state.

Although none of the choices sounded great, my intuition told me the last was the better option. We walked across the highway and within seconds a late-model car, driven by a friendly looking woman, pulled over. We climbed in, and she proceeded to tell us she had a flat tire earlier in the day in Reno and was rescued by a Good Samaritan. All day she had been looking for a way to pay back her "Karmic debt." She drove us all the way back into Mojave and dropped us off at a gas station. By then, it was midnight.

Just as we arrived, the gas station mechanic happened to be stopping by to pick up his paycheck. We learned that his home was near where our car broke down. "I'd be more than happy to drive you back and take a look at your car," he offered graciously. Taking us to the spot, he looked under the hood of the vehicle and announced, "You're in trouble! We can't do anything about this tonight." With that, he invited us to stay at his house until morning.

At 9:00 a.m. the next day he had the car towed back to the gas station. The crew of mechanics decided the damage was too complex for them to fix without putting in a new engine. We were about to call a tow truck to get us home when our friendly mechanic said, "Christian, my children have never seen the beach. How about if I tow your car with my truck and take the kids?" He didn't have to wait long for our reply. We rented a trailer hitch, got in his car and drove the two hundred miles back home to Ventura.

On the way, I had time to reflect on what had happened. I remembered how frantic I was when the engine blew, how apprehensive I felt about hitchhiking. I forgot that all I needed to do was quiet my mind, trust, and let Spirit do the work.

I thought of a statement by Swami Yogananda: "The mind's capacity is infinite. Therefore, if you think deeply enough about a subject, the answer to any question will come to you."

When I'm out surfing and my mind is filled with fear that the next wave is going to come crashing down in front of me, spinning me around like a crow in a tornado, it's impossible to be present in the moment where Spirit speaks. Even in wild times there are gaps or lulls between the action, allowing you to catch your breath and restore your perspective.

When your mind is racing with thoughts such as, "How am I going to fix this? I don't know what to do," you leave no room for Spirit to work its magic. When your brain is filled with "things I need to accomplish today because I didn't get them done yesterday," you leave no room for the Divine Presence to show you a quicker, easier way. You must clear the crowds out of your head and take the time to drop out of worldly cares. Sit in the space between the waves and regain your connection.

Surfing has taught me many spiritual lessons, including trust, abundance and unity. For the most part, I just go out to the ocean to get wet. All my everyday concerns stay on shore, left behind for as long as I choose. I think about how long it takes one wave to cross the sea, the rhythm of the tides, and the continuous abundant flow of water. There's no room on my board for checkbooks, cluttered desks or calendars.

To suppose Universal Intelligence would want us in bondage would be to dishonor the Creator. It's ludicrous to believe this wonderful creative expression, the master who has given us choice, energy and wisdom, would create and then say, "Now be miserable." If we begin to honor and trust Spirit inside of us, it will lift us out of bondage to worry, fear and frustration. Then we can watch our outside world reflect the magnificence that is our rightful inheritance.

# Seven

# What the Whales Know

*When we give up our fear
to the Higher Power and allow
ourselves to be a channel for
the Divine Presence, it shows up!
Ernest Holmes talks about emotional
storms: "When we learn to trust
the universe, we shall be happy,
prosperous and well."
God is always God no matter what
our emotional storms may appear to be.
There is always something hidden in your
inner being that has never been violated.
We may stumble,
but there is always an internal voice
saying "ski" when the timing is right,
"surf" when the waves are perfect.*

# Chapter 7

# WHAT THE WHALES KNOW

## Trusting the Wave

As I was sitting out on the cliffs doing my morning meditation, I saw the first whale of the season heading south to warmer waters. Usually these magnificent animals show up once, spout and continue on their way. But this whale was very slowly moving his way down the coast. He'd dive down and come up, spout, lift his tail out of the water, then dive again. I watched him perform this ritual at least five different times, sitting there in awe of this majestic creature that was the epitome of spiritual expression.

I couldn't help but think about those years in Hawaii when the whales would begin to show up during the holiday season. For some reason, year after year, they would find their way to the very same spots, journeying to the little stretch of water between Maui and Lanai. Whales going down to the lagoons in Baja don't have as big a navigational decision to make; they just follow the coastline south until the water feels warm enough to stay.

But the whales in Hawaii migrate from Canada and Alaska. They travel over 5000 miles of ocean, with no directional signs, instruments or maps to guide them. Yet every year, they show up in the very same spot.

In Longboat Key, Florida, there's a man known as the "Pelican Man," whose mission in life is to care for sick and injured pelicans. He has done his job so well, the State of Florida gifted him a piece of its property along the coast. (Imagine being given a piece of prime coastal property.) Somehow, the injured pelicans out there in the keys and the gulf know this is a sanctuary for them. Each morning when the "Pelican Man" shows up to unlock the gates, all the injured pelicans in the neighborhood come to be healed.

How does this happen? I don't know—but I do know it's the same mind that can speak Whalese, can speak Pelicanese. One can't help but wonder about the intelligence within these creatures. There's a voice, a navigating system—something beyond our realm of conscious—a linguistically programmed, thinking mind that moves them forward to the right place. It is a spiritual expression. And these are whales and pelicans!

Think about your place in the scheme of nature. Judaic teachings call man "a little lower than the Gods." Having such a high status, wouldn't you agree that you must have access to the same spiritual voice that guides the sea creatures? You do! It is the still, small voice we speak of, the one, which resides within our beingness. Emerson called the voice, "teachings from within," and remarked, "Nobody yet has found the limit of its knowledge." In order to be able to receive these teachings, this direction, we have to be open to the gift and trust the giver.

If you want to learn the spiritual language, you must spend time in the ocean of the Presence. Take time in your daily preparation with Spirit. Make it as much a part of your morning routine as your hygiene regimen. Some people actually spend more time getting ready for the day by using their body enhancing routines and products than they do by morning meditation and prayer. If you want to be as in touch with your inner navigational systems as the whales are, you must spend time learning the language.

## In Sync With Spirit

Skiing is one of my great passions. I'm as comfortable in ski boots as I am in Reeboks. Seldom do I encounter situations on the mountain that absolutely challenge my faith and trust.

My friend Rob and I climbed onto the gondola in blowing winds and snow. With the weather dark and stormy, only a small trail left by the snowplows was visible. The gondola took us through the trees, up to the next chairlift. Not many people were skiing the peak Jupiter Bowl at over 10,000 feet that day. Rob and I got on the chair lift to climb higher and higher into the clouds, the wind almost pushing us back, straight down to the ground.

When we arrived at the top, we got off the lift, but instead of skiing down the bowl, we traversed across the mountain. In the nearby distance, another man was doing the same thing, but he suddenly stopped, took off his skis and began walking. "Hey, where are you going?" I called.

"I've been doing this for nine years," he called back. "Just follow me."

We went along, but found the trek very difficult. I'm not used to walking with heavy ski boots, carrying skis at 10,000 feet. Moving faster than we were, our fellow skier suddenly disappeared into the trees—nowhere to be seen.

It was pretty close to a white out. We stood there with the wind howling so hard it stood us straight up. Adrenaline coursed through our bodies as we realized we were stranded. "What should we do?" I asked.

"Let's go back," Rob suggested. But with near zero visibility, going back was impossible.

I was having great difficulty breathing, not certain

if it was the altitude or the anxiety. We stopped for a moment, sat down and I practiced some of my Yoga breathing techniques. I said to myself, "Breathe in twice, exhale four, breathe in three, exhale six..." My breathing calmed somewhat but my mind still wasn't calm. I needed to get myself centered. At times the simplest of methods work wonders.

I broke out some good Trader Joe's chocolate. The sweetness of the candy reminded me of the simple pleasures at home. My mind and body quieted down. Then I remembered my talk last Sunday; it was all about trusting the Spirit. I knew Spirit wouldn't have brought me up here to fail. I felt, "Yes, Christian, you're definitely in over your head, but not God's head." No matter how big the challenge, God is bigger. It doesn't matter if you're in a spot out of bounds, where there are no ski patrols and it's impossible for a rescue helicopter to land.

As soon as the calm replaced my anxiety, the storm subsided and the sun showed through a hole in the clouds, a shaft of light right on a sheer vertical crevice. Although conditions still weren't perfect, now was the time to ski down the mountain. A brief prayer filled my awareness. I felt the voice say the timing was right and jumped off, bursting through the wall of powder and landing in snow up to my chest. As I turned around, my buddy Rob came bursting through this big cornice of snow 10-15 feet exploding around him. Then the snow started tumbling down behind him like a little avalanche.

Our pulses quickened but it was obvious we were both in sync with Spirit. We raced down the hill, well in front of the cascading snow. As if by magic, the ray of light pointed to a clearing, which appeared right through the trees. We skied across the line out into the open field of untouched powder. It was absolute heaven!

### Trust in Yourself

When we give up our fear to the Higher Power and allow ourselves to be a channel for the Divine Presence, it shows up! Ernest Holmes talks about emotional storms: "When we learn to trust the universe, we shall be happy, prosperous and well." God is always God no matter what our emotional storms may appear to be. There is always something hidden in your inner being that has never been violated. We may stumble, but there is always an internal voice saying "ski" when the timing is right, "surf" when the waves are perfect.

Trusting Spirit begins with trusting ourselves. Most of us know what it is we want from life. Our intuition tells us the truth. But the sad part is most don't listen to the language of their intuition. Instead, they listen to the voice of this world. I've counseled with many people who have this challenge. "What do you want?" I ask.

"I don't know," they answer.

"If you don't know, who does?" I reply.

Often, pretending not to know what you want in life feels safer than speaking the truth. Just think what could happen if you told other people your goals and dreams.

Some might say, "Are you serious? You can't do that!"

Others might ask, "Are you sure that's what you want to do?"

Still others, attempting to land lock you into their small mindedness, may remark, "Why don't you get a real job instead of being such a dreamer?"

Their own fears and doubts are what make them criticize you. As Thoreau said, "Most people live lives of quiet desperation." They believe fate has handed them a pre-determined life of working hard, saving and scrimping for retirement and then death. Their lives are summed up in a popular bumper sticker that reads, "Life's a bitch, and then you die." Only a small percentage of the population are dreamers who believe they can have an even more bountiful, joyous life than the one they already have.

Others simply don't trust themselves. "What if I make a mistake?" If you make a mistake, so what? Being trusting and trustworthy doesn't mean being perfect. Making poor choices in your life only means you're human. Trustworthy means you're willing to be accountable for those mistakes, clean them up and not repeat the same ones. We're learning what the right choice is and how to go about creating its reality in our lives. Most situations we call "mistakes" are lessons we need to learn—mainly the lesson of cause and effect. When we put a cause in motion, it will always produce some kind of effect.

**A Causal Plane**

This law of cause and effect is evident throughout life, as are its lessons:

~ Put your finger on a hot stove and you'll get burned.
~ Walk out in front of a speeding truck and you'll get hit.
~ Eat sugars, fats, live a sedentary life and you'll get fat.
~ Jump off a cliff and you'll fall.
~ Stick your finger in a light socket and you'll probably be fried.

Children learn to stay away from hot stoves. Alert pedestrians look both ways before they cross the street and people who are concerned with their physical bodies begin to eat sensibly and do moderate exercise. People who don't have a death wish use hang-gliders when jumping off cliffs and a plug when dealing with electric outlets. The law of cause and effect is ever dependable.

Some lessons we learn quickly, but others we continue to forget. Nature has its own immutable laws: the Illinois River can flood out Peoria when the torrential rains come; houses built on steep hillsides may slide after an earthquake or El Niño rains; and just as in the Wizard of Oz mobile homes could be picked up and tossed about, should a powerful tornado blow through town. None of these occurrences happen because God is angry with us. We have just gone against natural laws of nature.

Cause and effect is always evident in the ocean. You see a huge wave that seems to come from nowhere and crashes down in front of you. You're looking at ten or twenty feet of white water that's about to engulf you. It's not necessary to figure out what Karmic debt you're being asked to pay back. You needn't try to remember what you said wrong to your mate. It's not about anything you've done wrong. It's just that when you're fully participating in either life or surfing, there are going to be some outside, unexpected waves—this is the natural law of nature. If I want to play in God's swimming pool, I must not take it personally when it happens. The lesson for you is how to handle these difficult situations. Should you pull back in life or continue to risk and trust? Will you allow yourself to get sucked into the collective wave, or dive beneath the chaos to where it's calm?

One afternoon, Kalli and I were walking through the canyons of Del Mar, when two snarling German

Shepherds, their teeth bared and eyes demonic, charged directly towards us from the other side of the hill. I thought, "Okay, Christian. You can either trust or run." Since I run faster than my wife, I realized that running wouldn't have been a healthy choice for our relationship.

Off in the distance we heard a voice yelling, "Hey, come here." One of the dogs darted off. The other one continued to move towards us but seemed calmer. I could see the hackles on his back receding and his eyes soften as I knelt down and spoke, "Hey, buddy, nice dog." As I continued to speak, my voice relaxed him even more. My decision to trust instead of run was the right one.

When we have faith and trust in the Power within us, we'll watch our personal universe reflect its magnificence and come to realize our world is right and just. The difficulties we encounter are simply the opportunities to bring forth Spirit in a greater way. Don't dwell on the difficulties or challenges in a relationship, the physical handicaps or people who wronged you. Concentrate, instead, on allowing Spirit to move through you in wondrous ways. Put Spirit first in all things. Only then will you overcome and be greater than you were before.

Gandhi was thrown off trains and spent nights in jail because his skin was the wrong color. He used those experiences to give him the inner strength to lead millions of people to freedom.

When Moses was born, an edict from the Pharaoh ordered all the male infants to be killed. To protect her son, Moses' mother carefully put him in a basket and sent him floating down the river. Imagine the counseling he would have gone through if that happened today. But Moses didn't end up on a talk show. Instead, he grew up to lead the children of Israel to the Promised Land.

What is your higher voice encouraging you to do when you see the outside wave on the horizon?

## The Legacy of Joseph

One of the greatest success stories comes from the Bible. Joseph, born one of twelve brothers, was his father's favorite son. Joseph had a dream showing him he would be the one to lead the tribe and inherit the family's legacy. Jealousy finally overtook the brothers when Joseph flaunted his coat of many colors, the kind all noblemen wore, which his father had given him as a gift.

To get back at Joseph, his brothers decided to get rid of him. First they tried to kill him by throwing Joseph into a pit. There he was, the chosen child, at the bottom of a deep, dark hole. He began to pray. Rather than getting into blame, he looked inside of himself asking, "What can I do to become the leader I am meant to be?" He knew God wasn't out to get him, but looked at his misfortune as an opportunity to grow. He remembered who he was to be, a leader of men. Trusting Spirit, Joseph knew being in the pit was only temporary. What kinds of thoughts race through your mind when you are in the pits of life? Whom do you blame when a wave of difficulty crashes down on you?

Joseph's brothers decided to sell him to a tribe of Ishmaelites for twenty pieces of silver. They returned home, carrying Joseph's coat and told their father his favorite son had been killed. Meanwhile, Joseph had been sold to one of the top Ishmaelite generals. He was no longer in a pit, but a servant in a palatial mansion. Soon he became the head servant, running the house during the general's frequent absences.

One evening while the general was gone, his beautiful wife tried to seduce Joseph. He was extremely tempted. This was not an easy situation for a seventeen-year old guy to manage. But he stood fast and refused her advances. Feeling scorned, the general's wife accused the young man of rape and had him thrown into another pit—the dungeon.

The lows in life give us the understanding and the strength to remember who we are. These times give us the opportunity to test our belief and faith that Spirit has only ultimate good in store for us. From the lowest point in Joseph's life, he developed the consciousness that would lift him above his physical circumstances.

One night, the Pharaoh's cook and butler were thrown into the dungeon because they had angered their master. They had heard Joseph possessed the ability to interpret dreams. The cook told him of his dream, and Joseph offered his interpretation: "You will be kept here for thirteen days," he said, "then released." Next Joseph told the butler, "This dream means the Pharaoh will send for you tomorrow." Both of the predictions came true. Before they left, Joseph asked them to plead for his release. They agreed, but promptly forgot. There in the dungeon he remained, all the time praying and trusting he would be released and take his rightful place.

Two years later, the Pharaoh had a disturbing dream. "I need someone to tell me what this means," he bellowed. The butler, who was in the same room, told his master of the young man in the dungeon who had interpreted his dream while the butler was imprisoned. Joseph was summoned immediately.

Pharaoh related his dream to Joseph, who told him, "This means you will have seven great years of lush harvests and feasting, followed by seven years of famine. You should begin to put some of the harvest away to take care of you and your people later." The master was so impressed, he appointed Joseph as his right hand man. His job was to oversee the storing of food the first seven years, and the distribution over the next seven.

Fourteen years passed, and once again Joseph's predictions were accurate. Famine ravaged the countryside and people from all over the land came for food. One day, a group of eleven men appeared and bowed before Joseph. He recognized them as his brothers, but didn't say a word, nor did he take advantage of his important position. Instead, Joseph told his assistants to put extra food into the bags of his brothers and also put the money back in their sacks. He had finally grown into the leader his dream had shown him he would be.

Without the experiences of the past, Joseph would have lacked the necessary qualities of leadership: patience, tolerance, compassion and trust. Through his dark nights, he lifted up his heart and mind to Spirit. He never once doubted his legacy and birthright.

Joseph never forgot who he was, even when his world looked bleak. He knew his divine purpose was to be a leader out in the light of day, not in a dark dungeon. The reality his brothers saw for Joseph was not the language he was being guided by.

Not all stories of triumph over adversity come from ancient history. Modern-day spiritual warriors are prevalent as well. One such hero is a young Air Force pilot.

## Rescued by God

Capt. Scott O'Grady was flying a mission over Bosnian Serb territory. Somehow his F-16 found its way into a "no fly zone." Suddenly a ground to air missile fired a direct hit at his aircraft and cut it in half. O'Grady had less than twenty seconds to eject. He reached for what he later called "the beautiful gold handle," and blasted himself out of the plane—26,000 feet over hostile territory. As he plummeted towards the ground, he cried out, "Dear God, my fate is in Your hands!"

Ground visibility wasn't too good, and his descent took him directly over a main highway in the city. So as he floated slowly closer to the ground, O'Grady noticed crowds of people looking straight up at him. "I thought they were standing there, waiting for me," he remarked.

Landing in a dense forest, he scurried towards a thick growth of bushes. His next move was to camouflage himself as fully as possible, hiding his face by digging it into the ground and covering his ears with green gloves. Within four minutes the Serbs swarmed the forest and sprayed the area with bullets. "I was just praying they wouldn't see or hear me," O'Grady said.

Back in Alexandria, Virginia, his family was praying as well. The day after his son was shot down, Dr. William O'Grady received a typewritten message that read, "Your son was in Bosnia and his plane was destroyed by enemy fire. No one saw him eject and we have received no signal from him."

Capt. O'Grady carried eight, 4oz. water packs with him, but no food. He subsisted on leaves, grass and ants. Once the water was gone, he caught rainwater in a Ziploc bag. The only other piece of equipment he had was a survival radio, about the size of a Walkman. He searched for the perfect location to signal his compatriots at home—a clear, high point from which to broadcast, with a spot for helicopters to land, and, most importantly, it could not be too visible.

After six days, the NATO personnel heard, "Basher-52 reads you. I'm alive! Help!" They weren't sure if the signal came from their pilot or the Serbs, but they didn't hesitate.

At sunrise the next morning, two Stallion helicopters, two gun ships and two jets arrived at O'Grady's location. He saw them coming and sent up a flare. Twenty marines secured the area around him. The helicopter door opened and within three seconds, a sobbing but grateful Scott O'Grady jumped in.

Later that afternoon, he held a news conference at Aviano Air Force Base in Italy. The young hero couldn't figure out why he was getting so much attention. He'd just been doing his job. The very first thing O'Grady did was to thank God, "If it wasn't for God's love for me, I would never have made it. He's the one who delivered me here."

"How did you occupy your mind?" the newsmen asked.

"I prayed to God and asked him for a lot of things," he began, "and he delivered throughout the entire time. When I prayed for rain, he gave me rain. One time I prayed, 'Lord, let me at least have someone know I'm alive and maybe come rescue me.' That night T.O. (Hanford) came up on the radio."

He told the reporters there were dozens of times when the soldiers came within three feet of him. "How could they not see you?" the reporters asked.

"God," O'Grady replied.

Our Bible hero, Joseph, did not buy into the reality his brothers saw for him. Neither would Scott O'Grady believe his situation was hopeless, despite the odds stacked against him. They both knew as long as they fixed their thought and faith on God, Spirit would not let them down. Do you allow your fears to be the language of your mind, or do you choose to listen to your spiritual navigation?

At times, we all find ourselves in precarious, unplanned situations. Most of us have had some adversity in our lives. And if we believe in the law of cause and effect, we may have asked, "How did I get myself into this mess?" The answer to that question is, "Because we're always working on the never ending process of growing and becoming." Growth is not only about going to a weekend seminar for the "rah, rah, hype me up" stuff and coming out spiritually evolved. It's not about being ready to walk on water or over hot, smoldering coals after a five-day, intensive workshop.

Spiritual evolvement is a lifelong process and so is the consciousness that allows us to move further and further towards our good. The Buddhists believe they can spend ten thousand lifetimes working on just one of their noble truths. As spiritual beings we must not get caught up in the day-to-day littleness and difficulties, which may arise. We are continuously offered these opportunities to reflect upon our growth and character. We need to continue to remember who we are—"just a little lower than the Gods."

## Of Royal Birth

There's an old Sufi story about an Emperor who was

fed up with his only son. The father didn't approve of the young man's lifestyle and lazy habits, so he ostracized him from the kingdom. Isn't it interesting to note truths have no expiration date? Many of today's parents feel the same way about their offspring.

"Out you go," ordered the Emperor. Born of noble birth, the young man wasn't very handy with the basic trades needed to survive in the world, so he became a beggar. He carried his bowl around and begged with the others on the streets, but didn't quite fit in. Even after several years, the young man's walk was still princely, though he had long forgotten he was a prince, entitled to the kingdom.

When you have tasted the nectar, experienced the kingdom of the Spirit and suddenly you're disconnected, life becomes very painful. There is a longing to go back, but the fear or knowledge that you can't seems to turn off any remembrance. The Emperor's son consciously shut the inner voice and feeling off for the next ten years and continued to beg.

One day his father said to one of his aides, "I'm getting old. I think I'm going to die. I guess it's time to forgive my son."

"We don't know where he is," the aide replied, "he's been gone so long."

But the Emperor ordered, "Go find him!"

Going out into the world looking for the boy, the aide wandered the streets for weeks. Finally, he spotted a young man who seemed to have the countenance and gait of royalty.

The aide walked up to the beggar and said, "Your father has called you back."

In that moment the son stood up straight and remembered who he was. "I am the Emperor's son," he declared. "Fetch me a horse, a bath and some new clothes. I am ready to go home where I belong."

There is something in us that knows we are all of royal birth. Trusting the Spirit doesn't necessarily give us what we want immediately. The morning dew can eventually dissolve iron and steel by rusting them away a little at a time. A drop of water can eventually move granite boulders. Be persistent in believing and trusting; the power dwells within you. Spirit is always with you, even though sometimes you think it's not.

An anonymous poet writes:

> *One night a man had a dream.*
> *He dreamed he was walking along the beach with the Lord*
> *Across the sky flashed scenes from his life.*
> *For each scene he noticed two sets of footprints in the sand; one belonging to him and the other to the Lord.*
> *When the last scene of his life flashed before him, he looked back at the footprints in the sand.*
> *He noticed that many times along the path of his life there was only one set of footprints.*
> *He also noticed that it happened at the very lowest and saddest times in his life.*
> *This really bothered him so he questioned the Lord about it.*

*"Lord, you said that once I decided to follow you,
you'd walk with me all the way.
But I've noticed that during the most troublesome
times of my life, there is only one set of footprints. I
don't understand why, when I needed you most you
would leave me."
The Lord replied, "My precious, child, I love you
and would never leave you.
During those times of trial and suffering, when you
saw only one set of footprints,
it was then that I carried you."*

The voice, guiding the whales, pelicans, Gandhi, O'Grady, the prince and Joseph, is in you. You must trust life and keep your heart open. Trust your feelings and emotions to let you know how you really feel. Within you is the dwelling place of the most high. All of the mystics— including Moses, Jesus, Buddha, Lao Tsu, Krishna, Mohammed—all talked about that indwelling presence that is always with you. Remember this, call it forth and it will bring you wondrous gifts.

# Eight

# God and Money

*You were placed upon this earth for
a Divine purpose. The performance
of that purpose is what will bring
you happiness. Learn to tune
into whatever you should be doing.
Allow your mind and thoughts to be filled
with Spirit and you'll begin to notice
unlimited possibilities.
You'll discover your Divine Mission
in life. Two-foot waves are not the big stuff,
but going out, busting loose and having fun
with what's at foot creates a joyous
consciousness that thrusts one
into living their dream.*

# Chapter 8

# GOD AND MONEY

In the classic surfing movie, Endless Summer, two friends traveled around the world for a year, following the waves. In Africa they surfed places where no one before them had ever surfed. At one point they came to an astounding conclusion: "These waves must have been breaking on this beach for thousands of years." What a graphic example of the unlimited abundance of our universe. Out in the ocean, it doesn't matter if you've just missed a great wave. You know nature brings thousands more to you, an unlimited supply, every single day.

Catherine Ponder, a famous writer of prosperity books repeats frequently, "God is the Source of our supply. If we can remember that one phrase, we'll find more abundance in our lives." We often think people, jobs or other outside influences are our Source. It's important to remember they are only channels for God to work through.

Moses told the Israelites, "Remember, it is the Lord our God who gives you the power!" Spirit gives us the power to be able to receive wealth; but people allow themselves to slip into the mass consciousness that worries about rent and car payments. They think more about money than they think about God. How often have you recently:

~ thought about money?

~ engaged in conversations around dollars?

~ felt anxious and fearful about unpaid bills?

One doesn't need to go to God for things, for healing or for whatever. What is essential is to go to God for God and all else is added.

How much more (or less) time did you spend thinking and talking about God? To which do you dedicate your life more, looking for the wealth of continuous waves or looking for proof they're no good or not enough? If you feel less than prosperous, look at your thoughts and conversations. See which subject gets more time, money or God.

John was a hard working laborer who was referred to me for counseling. He told me his marriage was in trouble, because he and his wife were constantly battling over unpaid bills. "I don't believe I've ever seen you at church, John," I said. "Oh, no, Reverend. We don't have time for church." I asked him how often he and his family talked about God stuff or prayed together. His answer was, "Never." He also told me he hated his job and wanted to do something else. John had two challenges: First, his money-God ratio was out of balance, and second, he wasn't working at a job he felt called to do. He needed to put Spirit back into his life and do some soul-searching as to how he could be happy earning a living.

You were placed upon this earth for a Divine purpose. The performance of that purpose is what will bring you happiness. Learn to tune into whatever you should be doing. Allow your mind and thoughts to be filled with Spirit and you'll begin to notice unlimited possibilities. You'll discover your Divine Mission in life. Two-foot waves are not the big stuff, but going out, busting loose and having fun with what's at foot creates a joyous consciousness that thrusts one into living their dream.

Life wasn't going well when Londoner, William Booth went out to the hillsides. He carried a bible with him, opened it up and began to pray. "God, I may not be the most courageous person on this planet, nor have the most ability. I do not even possess great intelligence. But I commit right now I will give you William Booth's full intelligence, courage and ability." He sat on the hillside for hours, praying and waiting for a message from on high. Finally, he received the guidance he sought. Booth came back to the streets of London a changed person. Booth began to share his ministry until it grew to cover England, all of Europe and over to the United States. Today, the Salvation Army ministers to millions of people throughout the world. William Booth's life was a perfect example of someone searching for, discovering and following his Divine Purpose.

Pete used to be the top salesman at the local Nissan dealership. Two years ago, his son Sean was born. Pete called me and asked for assistance and prayer work. "I used to be excited about going to work. Now, when I'm there, all I can think of is I want to be at home with Sean. I can't eat, because at work I've been sick to my stomach. My sleep is disturbed with nightmares about losing my boy. And I'm not making money because neither my mind nor my heart is there. What should I do?" Pete knew what he needed to do. He left his job at the car lot and found a way to work at home on his computer. In the first month he earned almost what he had been earning as a car salesman. More importantly, he's home when Sean wakes up, has time to play with him during the day and usually tucks him in at night.

Don't fool yourself. If you are working to pay bills only and your heart is somewhere else, you'll never be successful. Move towards what you know satisfies your inner being and you'll find those untouched waves of abundance at your feet. For when you commit yourself to Spirit, there will be no lack or limitation in your life. Unfortunately, humankind often slips into the concept of scarcity.

There is no scarcity in the Universe. As Ernest Holmes wrote, "The Universe is abundant, unlimited in every respect; if it were not unlimited it would have depleted itself long, long ago." If there is so much abundance, why do we find this so hard to believe? Mainly because we tend to live our lives based on past experiences or the lessons we were taught growing up. We tend to slip into the collective hypnotic trance of the tabloid consciousness.

## A Slice of the Pie

~ There's just so much coconut cream pie on the table. What if someone takes more than one slice? There won't be enough for the rest of us.

~ If John gets the job, there won't be one for me.

~ All the good men/women are already taken.

Did parents who went through The Great Depression over fifty years ago raise you? You may have inherited some of their fears such as:

~ I'd better hang onto what I have. I could lose all of it any day now.

~ Don't get so comfortable. Things are too good to last. We are told to live in the moment, yet very often we get stuck in the past, especially when we're reminded of hard times.

~ I remember when there wasn't enough of anything on the grocery shelves. That's the reason I buy ten boxes of cereal at one time.

~ Always keep your gas tank filled to the top. Remember when we had to wait in long lines because of the shortage.

New stars, comets and even whole galaxies are being discovered all the time. There's always an abundance of puppies and kittens at the animal shelters. The power and intensity of love does not lessen if it is split between two or six children. There is always more to go around, whether it's love, puppies or money. For some reason, many of us are sure there's a shortage of green pieces of paper with pictures of dead U.S. Presidents on them.

Our government prints millions of dollars everyday. Passed around, it stays in circulation from one to five years. When it becomes faded and torn, money is replaced. Unfit currency is sent to the Federal Reserve Bank for destruction and replacement. Buildings crumble, cars go to wrecking yards, clothes disintegrate, but money is one of the only commodities that is always replaced. There is no shortage. And today you don't even have to hold the dollar bills in your hand. With computers, billions of dollars move through the information highway twenty-four hours a day. Do you still want to believe in shortage, or would you like to plug in and enjoy your rightful share?

One of the reasons the supply of money is never depleted is because it is constantly being re-circulated. The parable of the talents is a fine example. A man has three servants. To each one of them he gives some talents (money), saying he is testing them but not explaining how. When he returns from his voyage, he asks the first servant how many talents he has. The servant shows his master he has doubled his money through trading. The next one earned even more. But the third one still had the one talent he was given. He told his master he was being careful, for fear of losing the money. In fact, he did lose his money. The master called the servant a lazy sloth, because he did not circulate what was given him. Then he took the money from the frightened man and gave it to the richest one. The lesson of the parable and of life is this: give and it shall be returned to you many times over. Hold back on giving, hold onto your good and the universe will react in kind.

The monkey hunters in Indonesia know how important it is to let go. They use the knowledge to catch their prey. The hunters find large gourds, the ones that are big on the bottom but have a thin neck. They cut off the tops, drop pebbles into the gourds and then wait. Within minutes, several monkeys gather around, curious about what's in the gourd. They stick their little hands into the thin neck. As soon as the hunters know the monkeys have grabbed a few pebbles, they surround the animals. The monkeys want to get away, but can't pull their hands out while they hang onto the pebbles. In hanging onto their treasure, they lose their freedom.

Our environment also teaches us lessons about letting go. When the natural rhythm of nature is interrupted and blocked, whole eco-systems suffer. My parents used to take me to a vacation ranch where there was a wonderful pond with fish, lilies grew around the outskirts and frogs inhabited the shores. What a magical place for a young boy to enjoy. A number of years later, I went back to the ranch and was horrified to see that the pond had died. There used to be a wonderful stream flowing in and out of the pond, a circulation that gave it life. Then the stream got dammed up. The pond began to stagnate. The fish and plants died. It was no longer a living organism.

In what ways are your beliefs blocking the infinite flow? Do you really think your relatives, your employer or your bank are your source of life and abundance? Are you hanging onto the pebbles of resentment, anger or other toxic feelings? These emotions may be keeping you from your good. Are you damming up your channels of acceptance by looking outside for the answer?

## Look to the Source

GOD IS YOUR SOURCE, not your employer.

Jean worked at a small company for two years. She put in extra hours without pay and was promised a raise several times, never receiving the increase. She was having trouble meeting her monthly bills, but was afraid to ask her boss for a raise. "What if he refuses? What will I do?" It was as if Jean had blinders on to any other avenue of income except this particular CEO. She didn't even bother to seek out other jobs in her field.

Instead of worrying about whether or not you'll get a raise in salary, why not go directly to your wellspring? Emma Curtis Hopkins, the metaphysical "teacher of teachers," tells us if we go directly to the source, we need not worry, beg, beseech or limit. Just affirm with conviction, "Give us this day, our super, substantial bread," says she. The flow of Spirit is always far greater than any worldly flow.

GOD IS YOUR SOURCE, not the ATM machine.

Isn't it amazing how we can put a little piece of plastic in a cement wall and have money come out? But have you ever noticed people's attitudes about those shiny, mechanical monsters when the money doesn't appear? Watch how sane, intelligent men and women stand in front of computerized ATM machines and yell at them when money doesn't show. They blame the inanimate ATM machine, especially when their card gets eaten and the machine won't give it back. Granted, sometimes ATMs can malfunction, but most of the time the person has messed up. They've either put the wrong PIN (pain in the neck) number in, or lost track of their checking account balance. ATM machines do not keep your money without good cause. Neither does God withhold your good from you as long as you do your part. Your task is to acknowledge God as your source and trust the process to work.

Michael, a young chiropractor, shared with me how he struggled in the early days of his career. The job took up too many hours for him to devote time to his family. When he was home, Michael was thinking about his job, not his wife and kids. Even though he knew his emotional absence would be short-lived, he felt guilty for not being fully there. His growing family also needed a nicer, larger house. Michael affirmed daily, "I know God is my source and my supply." Soon the thought became a part of his being. Within six months, his practice blossomed enough that he was able to cut back on his hours and buy a beautiful, new home. He says, "Each day I feel better and better about myself. Because I have no worries about money, my time and my mind are freed up." Presently Michael spends three days a week at home, being the kind of husband and father he always wanted to be.

Abundance is a natural state of being; poverty is not. The best thing you can do for the poor is not to be one of them. The universe is not impoverished and neither are you. In the book, "Good Cents," Stephanie Sorensen and I recommended, "Open your eyes. Picture yourself taking a walk along the beach and feel your feet sink into the soft, cool sand. How many grains of earth do you suppose move and shift with each step? You watch pelicans dip into the water for their evening meal. Do they ever come away hungry because there are not enough fish? You couldn't even count the number of sandpipers scurrying to the shore, or the sea gulls looking for their dinner. The universe is alive with abundance!" Such awe-inspiring moments are but mini-fragments of the bountiful picture of life. You, as an integral part of the universe, are entitled to share in this cornucopia of wealth.

Our old beliefs about wealth are some of the factors that keep us from participating in the abundance of our world. In Marcia Hootman's work, I'd Rather Be Rich, she asks, "Have you ever said...
~ I'd rather be happy than rich
~ Money can't buy happiness
~ The more money you get, the more you want
~ I'm into spirituality, not money..."
   These beliefs have been in your psyche since childhood. Ask yourself some telling questions:
~ What does the word "money" mean to me?
~ What kinds of feelings does the word "money" bring up in me? (fear, excitement, anxiety, disgust, etc.)
~ What did my parents teach me about money?
   Change the word "money" to love, joy, passion, energy, nurturing relationships or health. It's all spiritual energy given another name. So if you are experiencing lack in any of these areas, you need to get in and clean out your old, limiting beliefs. Awareness is the first step to solving a problem or changing any unwanted situation.

Once you've become aware of your beliefs, two more questions are necessary to begin changing your life:
1. Are these beliefs and attitudes valid for me today?
2. Do I want to keep them or change them?

### Imagining Your Good

Just as there are untold waves to ride from places never before seen, so there are untold ideas waiting to be discovered. So many believe all the places to ride have been conquered and all ideas have been expressed, but these limiting thought just aren't true.

One of the most effective ways of changing old belief systems is through visualizing new ones. Emmet Fox claims, "The secret of successful living is to build up the mental equivalent that you want, and get rid of...the mental equivalent that you do not want." If certain limiting attitudes and beliefs continually run through your mind, replace them with a belief in abundance. The physical brain does not know the difference between what we vividly visualize and what we actually see.

Marjorie and Tom were married during World War II. They wed the night before he left for overseas duty in Europe. Even though they spent their first two years apart, they were very much in love and committed to being together for the rest of their lives. Tom and Marjorie kept their commitment to the very last moment.

Three years ago, the whole family decided it was time for the couple to let go of the large home they occupied. They moved into a retirement home just outside of town, right on the coast. Several months ago, Tom took ill and the doctors' prognosis was not good. Marjorie insisted on moving into the room with her husband.

Her bed sat close to the window. Tom, who could hardly sit up, would ask Marjorie to describe the scenery. "Oh, Tom, it's beautiful," she would say. "You can see the whitecaps rolling onto the shore. There are people skating, riding bikes and walking on the boardwalk like we used to. Only they're wearing those neon colored shorts that would probably glow in the dark. Looks like a nice breeze is blowing, 'cause I can see the trees kind of swaying back and forth." Everyday she would let Tom know what was happening outside the window. You could just see his eyes light up at his wife's vivid descriptions.

One day while Marjorie was walking out in the corridors, Tom was being wheeled down to radiology. Before they left the room, he told his attendant, "Take me over to the window. I want to see for myself." The man obliged and pushed Tom towards Marjorie's bed. "Pull back the curtain," Tom instructed. The attendant slowly reached for the curtain, began to pull it back and they both gasped. The only thing you could see from this window was the brick wall of the hospital's next wing. Marjorie, wanting to please her beloved, had made up all the pictures. Tom, not knowing, could see every tree, each person, all the colors she had described. In his mind, the scenery was real.

Athletes routinely use visualization to improve their performance. Olympic slalom skiers see themselves going through each and every gate, safely and smoothly. Former Olympic gymnast, Marylou Retton said she had seen her gold-medal winning dismount over a thousand times before she actually jumped off the vault.

Surfers stand on the beach for hours, watching how the waves break and critiquing other surfers. They read articles about surfing and watch movies about surfing. In riding a wave, you have to be spontaneous, move instantly and naturally without thinking. There are many steps involved in the process; too many to concentrate on once you're in the water. Visualizing the ride embeds these steps deeply into the subconscious mind, where it becomes second nature. Surfers so fully visualize the experience of living and breathing the ride, their minds, hearts and souls are fully saturated with the feeling. They can taste the salt on their lips and hear the sound of the wave's crumbling lip. They can feel the water spray on their faces and the rush of being lifted up by a ten-foot wave, then the thrust and momentum of the water pushing them swiftly towards shore. This is how vivid your visualization needs to be. You want to incorporate all your senses: smell, taste, hearing, sight and touch. I have used the visualization process to achieve numerous desires in my life. One of my most powerful manifestations was my home in Hawaii.

The price of the homes near the church started at about a million dollars each. Those kinds of dollars were beyond my wildest imagination at that time. The credit cards had been maxed out to ship everything across the ocean and escrow on the Ventura home had not yet closed. In fact, things were even worse, the sale we thought was solid had just fallen out of escrow.

Regardless of what appeared to be a futile attempt, we went looking for the perfect house. There is a beautiful town called Kaaawa, just past Chinaman's Hat, nestled directly under the rock formed and world-renowned restaurant called by the name, "The Crouching Lion." Streets lined with gorgeous palm trees, tropical breezes, the town had everything you envision when you think old Hawaii.

We found an exquisite two-story house, nestled in the jungle, overlooking the ocean. Two gigantic waterfalls cascaded from the cliffs in the backyard. All around the perimeter of the house sweeping balconies stretched out to the sea.

The owners had been trying to put together some kind of business deal in Europe. They weren't quite sure if or when this would take place. Even though we didn't have immediate access to the money needed to buy the house, we decided it was going to be ours. In talking to the owners, we discovered that the mortgage was held privately. This was good news since a lending institution would not have looked fondly on my present financial situation, particularly since I had no job other than the beginnings of a ministry.

Each day I would sit out on the cliffs overlooking the bay and visualize myself in that house. I walked through all the rooms hundreds of times in my mind. I saw myself drinking a hot cup of Kona Coffee, sitting on my bedroom balcony watching the dolphins play in the surf. I felt the cool tiles beneath my feet as I wandered through the corridors, barefooted. I paddled out with the sea turtles and surfed the waves directly in front of the house. In my meditations, I asked Spirit to show me whether or not this house was for my highest good. My spiritual self would accept the answer, but my human self really wanted this house!

Our real estate agent from the mainland called and said a family had moved into our house in Ventura on a lease option. They put down a substantial deposit and said they would buy the property within a year.

The owners of the Kaaawa house suddenly decided

to open an escrow with us, still not knowing whether they were going to leave the islands. I paid them a small deposit, opened escrow and waited. Five weeks later they called and said, "Christian, we have to be in Europe in two weeks. Go talk to the private mortgage holder and tell him you want to take over the payments."

"Do you know what that means?" I thought, "It means they don't want any money down. Thank you Father!"

I sat down with the mortgage holder and together we reviewed my TRW credit report.

"Christian, we'd be crazy to let you take over these payments. You're heavily in debt, your house has not yet sold and you've just started a new church."

"We're ministers," I protested. "We'll pay."

"We'll have to think about this one," he said, looking more skeptical than I would have hoped.

The next day our tenants in Ventura called and informed us they wanted to buy the house immediately. We returned to the mortgage holder with the good news and put the whole deal together. Our Ventura escrow closed within a week. We paid off our back debts, took over the house and moved in. Before the year was up, Hawaiian real estate prices jumped a whopping 45%. We refinanced our house, pulled out $50,000 and were once again financially solvent.

Scarcity is an attitude of the world. Abundance is of God. Don't give up your power to money or it will take the dominating part in your experience. Remember money is from God, a medium of exchange that Spirit has allowed us to discover and use. Without money, we would still be carrying pigs to the market to trade for the week's groceries. It is not money that is the root of all evil, but the love of money, or anything put before God, that is the problem.

God is your source, your personal and universal ATM machine that never says, "No." My relationship to God is the most important part of my life, for when I put Spirit first, I can handle any challenge, because I know Spirit is bigger than worldly problems. Don't tell God how big your problems are; tell your problems how big your God is. Once I get my littleness out of the way and know that I am a Divine avenue of Spirit, all the abundance of the universe is mine.

## Divine Timing

"Everything your heart desires will come to you," says Jiminy Cricket in the film, Pinocchio. This doesn't always mean immediately. There is something called "Divine Timing." Remember, Spirit looks at eternity. We look at the clock and the calendar. Often panic sets in when things don't happen according to our timing.

Our church has been looking for a site to build a new facility. We found what appeared to be the perfect place. However, the property is not zoned for churches. My financial officer called the City of San Diego and found out that a zoning variance could take as long as two years. We don't plan on moving anytime soon. But when I heard two years, I thought, "God, I don't want to wait that long!"

The Course in Miracles says impatience is when you think something won't happen. I don't have to worry about the zoning. If this is the right spot for us, the land will be zoned for and by God. The permits will be issued by the City of God, approved by Inspector God and the time required will not be my timing but Divine timing. If

I can just have "the faith of a mustard seed," as the Bible tells us, I can look out at the mountains of barriers around the site and say to them, "Be ye removed!"

At times we all face what seem like insurmountable challenges. Lack of cash flow, relationship problems, unemployment, or physical challenges can be overcome. Put Spirit first, develop a strong relationship with your Higher Power and you will be able to stand firm and face any challenge without fear or doubt. You have been given dominion over the birds, the fish, the creepy crawlers and worldly problems. It's up to you to exercise your power and know you are the Divine Presence speaking.

You have the capacity and the ability to think independent of conditions. But you must be willing to step out of the mass, collective consciousness and any inherited negativity. It has been said if you believe in suffering, you will suffer. What do you believe in? Which limitations have you accepted for yourself? Allow your thoughts to dwell upon abundance, not lack. Think health, not disease. And feel joy, not sorrow.

In his letter to the Philippians, the apostle Paul said, "Whatever is true...honest... just...lovely...of good report, think on these things." Don't concentrate on the newspaper headlines, the scarcity or negativity. These are just the dozen or so items somebody thought were important to let you know today. Why don't you choose what to think about? Reflect on God, the fullness and wholeness of the Spirit. Think about who you are. You are the conduit through which the Spirit comes into being. Remember: "The Lord is my shepherd, I shall not want."

Wouldn't it be great if you could remain at a high level of consciousness all the time? You can! Just follow Catherine

Ponder's first prosperity commandment that says, "Thou shalt look only to God as the Source of thy guidance and supply." Know, nothing but Spirit is your power, your strength and your source. Trust with all the faith you can muster. This energy will lift you out of challenges and guide you on the path to your highest good—to a new land with waves of opportunities never before witnessed.

*Nine*

# Catch the Spirit

*When so called "bad" things
happen, they may be just the
of newness. Our world is cyclical.
All life is recycled. Perennial plants lose
their leaves in the wintertime and bloom
once again in the spring.
Fur bearing mammals
(especially my cat and dog) shed their
coats in the summer and grow them back in
winter to protect them from the cold.
Organs donors have given new life to
thousands. What looks like destruction is
the beginning of something else. When we
have come to a time of completion in our
lives, it doesn't have to be negative.
Let go of sadness and move into a
wonderful new zest for living.*

# Chapter 9

# CATCH THE SPIRIT

## To Err is Human

Over the years I've made my share of what I'll call "poor wave selections." As a result, I've tumbled over the falls with no chance to recover, while the waves chewed up my surfboard as if it were a potato chip and held me down in a watery darkness until their was hardly any oxygen left in my blood. At those times, it was easy to blame myself for making a dumb choice—but the truth is it's part of surfing. And making weak choices is also part of spiritual evolution.

What is spirituality? Are we to accept Webster's definition, "pertaining to the spirit or its concerns as distinguished from bodily or worldly existence or its concerns." If so, being spiritual means having to deny ourselves the physical, earthly, sensual and material world. This is not the kind of tedious, humdrum existence Spirit intended for us. We are indeed spiritual beings but we live, move and breathe within a human body with human emotions and a human mind. This poses one of the most difficult dilemmas many of us have in following a spiritual path. Very often, we don't allow ourselves to be human.

We all make mistakes. The key is to learn from them and not to make the same ones over and over again. Human beings feel emotions such as anger, frustration, fear and worry. We overeat, procrastinate, pout, criticize and sometimes escape into the comfort of our beds and "blankies." What's important is that we don't beat ourselves up. Rather, we pick ourselves up. There is a saying, "Knock down seven times, get up eight."

I remember trying to learn how to roller-skate. The wheels kept going out from under me and I repeatedly fell down on my bottom or my elbows. I'd get back up, start again with arms flapping and a determined expression on my face. At first glance, I looked confident, but my ego was about to take over.

"Why couldn't I learn this as quickly as I picked up other sports?" I asked myself as I hit the ground one more time. My balance was great and my co-ordination flawless. "This isn't going well at all," I told myself. I allowed my ego and self-consciousness to get the best of me. That was the last time roller skates ever touched my feet.

Have you ever watched an infant take his first, tenuous steps? He takes one step, falls, takes two more, falls and repeats the process until one day he darts across the room. He hasn't yet learned the myth of perfection or adopted the habit of feeling self-conscious.

When I made the decision to give up roller-skating forever, I denied myself the right to a common, human frailty. I decided it was not okay to make mistakes. Of course, it wasn't long before my humanness got the best of me again and I made another mistake, then another. I had to learn mistakes were just part of living.

As a young boy, John played a game involving a stick and a stone. His favorite bat was a broom handle. He'd throw the stone in the air and swat it with his makeshift bat. The better the shape of the stone, the further it would fly.

One day, on his way home from school, John spotted what looked like the perfect stone. He couldn't wait to get home and grab the broom. Outside, ready to play, he could almost hear the crowd roaring. It was the bottom of the ninth inning, last game of the World Series. John flung the stone like a tennis pro ready to ace a serve. The throw was so perfect, the stone almost stopped in mid air. Wham! He hit it harder than ever before. He could almost see the crowd standing on its feet, cheering for him. What a magnificent moment! Until the rock went through the back windshield of his dad's brand new Buick Skylark.

There was a hole about an inch round, with glass shattered in a ray-like pattern all around. John's first thought was, "I'll run away from home and never come back." Being seven-years-old this was not a viable option—but crying was. He scrambled towards the house, tears running down his smudged cheeks, dragging the broom behind him.

John's dad was standing on the porch, watching the whole scene. He came out to the curb to meet the boy, put one huge hand on John's shoulder and said, "You know, son, you shouldn't have done that. It looks as if we're going to have to get a new window." That was it! In that moment, John saw his dad stand taller than ever before. He felt the pangs of guilt, but was happy his dad still loved him.

How many of us have shattered windows or upset lives and thought we deserved severe punishment? Know there is a heavenly father/mother God who is forgiving. Spirit holds no grudges against you. Why should you hold any against yourself?

## No Guilt Allowed

Guilt is the henchman of the ego. It is the executioner saying, "Find fault. See the bad and forget the good." Our ego thrives on attack. It pursues whomever it deems guilty, such as the person who "did it to us":

~ How could she do this to me? After all I've done!
~ Why didn't they invite me to their party?
~ Why did my boss promote her instead of me?

If there is no outside culprit to blame, the ego will tell us to attack ourselves:

~ Why didn't I handle this situation differently?
~ Why do I let them push my buttons?
~ How did I get myself into this mess again?

When something doesn't seem to be unfolding the way it should, let's not get our self-critical mind in there and say, "Look how I've blown it." Let us say instead, "How can I do this better next time." You can buy into guilt or see through to the innocence of the situation. "Forgive them (father), for they know not what they do." In Say Good-Bye to Guilt, Gerald Jampolsky tells us, "When we say 'good-bye' to guilt, we can then say hello to love." Don't allow guilt to obliterate love. For guilt is never the inner voice of wisdom, but of confusion.

## Beware the Bearers

Dr. Paul Brenner has commented that in the Jewish religion we learn guilt from our parents. Christians learn the concept from their religion. The notion of "original sin" begins the cycle of guilt. Preachers tell us we were born guilty. Then they quote scriptures, setting out doctrines for living. "You must obey the rules or else you have sinned." And sin brings punishment, if not in this world then in the next. Give me a break—one is not punished for their mistake but by them. And you are free when you stop sinning, or "mistaking."

In some religions, dancing will get you thrown into the fires of Hell and damnation. Others forbid alcohol, pork, music, soda pop or makeup. And should you lust in your heart, you will be doomed to hell for eternity. Just how long is eternity?

One preacher remarked, "Eternity is like the earth being a steel ball. Every million years, a dove grazes this sphere with its wings. When the steel ball wears down to nothing is when you'll be free." Now that's a long time!

Some followers are told all movies are bad. My friend, Jim took his children to see the Disney movie, Bambi. Jim's minister found out and told him he would be banished to hell for eternity. His description of eternity was even more threatening than the "steel ball" theory. "Think of a sparrow picking up one grain of sand and carrying it to the moon. He comes back, picks up another grain, and takes it to the moon. When the sparrow has removed every bit of dirt, when the earth has vanished, then you will be free." The Bhagavad Gita tells us, "When a man acts according to the law of his nature, he cannot be sinning."

Yet religions inflict guilt upon us in an effort to get us to behave. Our penal system follows suit. They believe putting a young thief in jail will change his behavior. Judging by the overcrowding of prison cells and the enormous recidivism rate, the system doesn't quite work. Yet we spend more money for incarceration than we do for education.

An exchange student from Korea graduated with honors from an Ivy League college and went on to medical school. One day, he walked down to the post office box to send a letter off to his parents in Korea. A bunch of gang members beat up, robbed and killed the young man. In Philadelphia, the city of brotherly love, there was instant outrage and a cry for swift justice. The perpetrators were taken into custody within days and arraigned on murder charges. They were teen-age boys.

The boy's parents came to the United States for the trial. They said nothing throughout the ordeal. The verdict came down as "Guilty." At this point the father asked permission to approach the judge's bench and kneeled before him. "Please have mercy on these boys who have been convicted," he told the judge. "They didn't have any family or education. The way of the streets is all they know. Give them to us. Let us raise them with love and teach them respect for life."

The reporters said there were tears running down the face of the judge as he leaned over to the boy's parents and apologized. "I'm sorry, sir, but it's not possible. Our justice system here doesn't work that way," he replied. The boys were sent to a state prison where they will spend most of their adult years, isolated from family, love and caring.

Parents can unwittingly administer generous doses of guilt, as well. A popular movie of the 1980s, Ordinary People, gave us a classic example. The movie was about a typical family of four—mom, dad and two sons. In one of the first scenes, the brothers were out boating on a lake. The younger of the siblings leaned over the side too far, fell into the water and drowned. Although his brother tried desperately to save him, he did not succeed. As a survivor, the boy took on the pain and horror of guilt.

Mom wasn't very helpful. Consumed with her own

grief, she didn't realize how harmful her words were to her remaining son. She would cry, "My favorite son is dead." This young teen was so wracked with guilt he fell into a deep depression, resulting in a suicide attempt. While recovering, he was interviewed by a sympathetic doctor. The physician asked him, "How did you come to feel so guilty?" The boy couldn't think of anything specific. He only remembered growing up he was taught when bad things happened, it was always somebody's fault. His brother drowned. Someone had to take the blame. Since he was the one there when the accident happened, the blame would have to fall on him.

We experience many symbolic deaths each and every day. Sometimes it's the end of a relationship. Perhaps you've been laid off from a job of twenty years. A closer look into the situation would probably prove nobody was at fault. People grow and times change. Whenever something ends, know it is the natural cycle of nature and life. No one needs to be made wrong. There are lessons to learn, growth to be had, and there is more than one personality involved.

## Letting Go

On the big island of Hawaii, Kilauea volcano has been erupting for almost ten years. At first glance, the devastation makes you feel very sad. Miles of rain forest are no longer present. Beautiful Artesian wells and hot springs are gone. Houses have been destroyed. The gorgeous resort community of Kalapapa is but a memory. Nearby roads are barren, the landscape looks like something out of prehistoric times and fog fills the air.

One night, I was watching the vibrant, orange lava

flowing. Five hundred billion tons of molten lava came out of the volcano each day. I noticed the land mass was increasing, along with the number of beaches built up by the volcanic eruption. As I thought about the changes, I realized all the islands of Hawaii were created in the same manner. Without volcanoes erupting, we would not have had the opportunity of experiencing the beauty we know as the Hawaiian Islands.

When so called "bad" things happen, they may be just the beginning of newness. Our world is cyclical. All life is recycled. Perennial plants lose their leaves in the wintertime and bloom once again in the spring. Fur bearing mammals (especially my cat and dog) shed their coats in the summer and grow them back in the winter to protect them from the cold. Organs donors have given new life to thousands. What looks like destruction is the beginning of something else. When we have come to a time of completion in our lives, it doesn't have to be negative. Let go of sadness and move into a wonderful new zest for living.

A Jewish proverb reads, "You will be punished in heaven for all the pleasure you have denied yourself on earth." Why deny yourself any pleasure, as long as it does no harm to anyone? Joy is the ultimate expression of God. Surfers know this. That's why there is no age limit to the sport. I've been in the lineup with middle-aged men, grandfathers and pre-teenagers. Once you get out into the waves, we all become as little children, enjoying the joyous gifts of nature. And who knows how to have more fun than kids?

## Spirituality is Joy

There's a fable about two children, Kirk and Luke,

who went to the park with their mom. The mother sat down on the park bench. Hide and go seek was the first game the kids played. Luke climbed up into a tree and hid. Kirk scrambled up after his brother. As children do, they began pushing one another. Luke lost his balance. Fearing his brother would fall, Kirk grabbed his shirt. Instead of falling, both the boys ended up flying through the air as if they had wings. They darted in and out of the trees in the park, flew amidst the fluffy, white clouds and back down to the park.

When the game was over, they went back to their mother. "Did you see us, mom?" they asked. "Yes, I did. And I was worried you would hurt yourselves. Let me show you the right way to climb a tree."

She walked them over to the tree and demonstrated. "You either keep two hands and one foot on the tree at all times, or two feet and one hand. In other words, never take more than one hand or foot off at a time. This way, you'll never lose your balance."

"But mom," the kids cried in unison, "if we hadn't lost our balance, we would have missed all the fun."

Have you given up your sense of adventure and play because you have learned the "safe" way to do things? Are you afraid to "err," to "tumble over the falls" of the wave, because you might be held down?

Playing is a natural part of all animal life. Even the animals in the wild know how to play. Monkeys swing through tree limbs at rapid rates. Dolphins ride the waves along with the best of surfers. Tigers and lions and bears play as long as they feel safe from predators. They're being who they are—carefree and playful. It's important for us to be who we are as well. As Diogenes said, "Man is the most intelligent of animals, and the most silly." Do you believe you were put on this earth to suffer or to be joyous? How many times do you play the game of life to win—or else?

At the University of Chicago, researchers studied two teams of athletes. The soccer team had low attendance, made no money for the school and had very little chance of winning. The other was the championship hockey team. They had to play for blood. To them winning was the only option. What the study found was the soccer players had better family lives, higher grades, fewer injuries and less stress than their counterparts.

When you play only to win, living becomes an attack, as opposed to an adventure. Winners are cheered and invited to victory celebrations. "Everyone loves a winner." And won't we do almost anything to belong, be a part of the crowd? In order to be accepted, we often go out of our way to please other people. Have you ever driven yourself crazy with imaginary thoughts about what others might be thinking of you?

### Spirituality is Forgiving Yourself

A group from our congregation went down to the Embarcadero in downtown San Diego, to see the Summer Pops concert. Jazz great Doc Severson was featured. We arranged to meet at 6:00 p.m. Being new to San Diego, I had never been downtown before, so I had intended to allow myself a little "getting lost" time. Unfortunately, the clock got away from me and I left late. Obsessed with being on time, my stomach started churning the minute I hit the freeway. The Convention Center adjacent to the Embarcadero was easy to find. Big, blue and bold, the facility stood out in the skyline of San Diego. But I didn't see any colorful signs reading, "Summer Pops this way," and there were no crowds milling about, carrying picnic baskets and blankets. I kept driving, turning up every side street, still having no clue where the parking lot was located. My insides by now were going a mile a minute. I could just hear the rest of my group, "Where's Christian? What a flake!" I finally found what looked like a good parking space.

"How do I get to the Pops?" I asked a fellow pedestrian. "You hop on a trolley." That's when I realized I was nowhere close to my destination. "Which trolley?" I asked.

"The one over there that's just pulling out. You'll have to wait another fifteen minutes for the next one." This was something I didn't want to hear.

"Stay calm, Christian," I reminded myself. I sat and waited, trying not to think about the anger and frustration inside of me. "They're going to be furious at me for being late. They're probably thinking I'm not going to show up." Of course, this was all I could think about for the next fifteen minutes. As scheduled, my trolley arrived and pulled up to the parking lot of the Pops ten minutes later. I walked through the entrance onto the open picnic ground. There was my group, having a great time. "Oh, hi, Christian," they waved. Nobody said a word to me about being late. They hadn't even noticed I was missing!

Why did I put myself through all the turmoil? Because a long time ago, I learned it was polite and proper to be on time. I didn't want the congregation to think I wasn't being polite and I certainly didn't want them to know their minister was human and got lost!

When we are out there struggling to be super human, worry and doubt slips in. Worry is believing things are not going to turn out okay or things didn't take place the way we thought they should have happened. "Should" is one of the most destructive words in our language.

## Freedom From "Shoulds"
Do you have one of those Aunt Mary's you should go visit? You know the one I mean. She's getting up in years, not feeling well and you know you should go see her. But something keeps getting in your way.

~ Are you still putting off going to the gym? You've been talking about taking off those extra pounds. You know you should start tomorrow!

~ When are you going to clean out the garage? You should have done it last spring.

I'm also guilty of "shoulding" on myself once in awhile. As a minister, my "shoulds" usually revolve around Sunday service.

~ I should have prepared more for this talk.

~ I should have got an earlier start.

~ I should have worked on my message, rather than go out.

~ I should have done more research.

~ I should have included more humor in the lesson.

You can have excuses or you can have results, but you can't have both. Had the talk been more important to me than my time out with friends, I would have stayed home. On this rare occasion, I chose to go out instead. As Wayne Dyer says, "You never shoulda, coulda, woulda. You either do or you don't." What good are the shoulds in your life? They are useless to the fulfillment of your dreams, desires or goals. The consciousness of "should" or "ought" will annihilate your victories.

Don't sit around oughting or shoulding on yourself, feeling guilty. Mae West said, "He who hesitates is last." When you don't take action, you miss out. Life is that simple! Throw those wish lists away. Wishing without follow up gets you nowhere. Take the steps necessary to achieve your dreams. And if you don't succeed immediately, if you fall back into being human, forgive yourself and begin again.

Forgiveness paints a picture of a world where suffering is over, loss becomes impossible and anger makes no sense. As Miguel de Cervantes said in Don Quixote de la Mancha, "There are no birds in last year's nests." Past events, whether they happened last year or a minute ago, have no power over you. Create the life you want, beginning now. Spirit has given you all that is necessary. Doubt not the gift and it is impossible to doubt its result.

As the old spiritual cliché goes, you are truly "a spiritual being having a human experience." For spirituality, like love is a verb. The depth of your personal spirituality is measured by how you live your life, day by day.

Are you willing to allow yourself to be human, to make mistakes?

Will you free yourself from the bondage of inappropriate guilt?

Do you recognize the significance of change, as in death and new life?

Can you be as a little child, overflowing with joy?

If you are willing to say "yes" to these questions, then you are on your way to living a more spiritual, more fulfilling life than you ever before imagined.

# Ten

# Barreled in
# the Wave

*Once when I was sitting up on*
*the cliffs, I was contemplating*
*the beauty of the day.*
*The rising sun was absolutely*
*gorgeous. Pink clouds reflected its rays.*
*All of a sudden, I almost felt myself*
*floating with the clouds, as they traveled silently*
*though the skies. I felt a oneness*
*with the rolling waves of the ocean.*
*My breathing felt in harmony*
*with the ebb and flow of the tides.*
*I noticed the grass rippling in the wind*
*before me in the same rhythm as my breath.*
*It all felt as if it were part of the same*
*vibration.*

# Chapter 10

## Barreled in the Wave

### The Heartland

When I gaze out upon the ocean, a calm surrender fills my soul. As I glide out into the surf and dive beneath my first wave, an instant merging with elements occurs. Carving across the face of a wave, like a machete through butter, causes all surf dreams to fade to the real experience as I become one with the rhythm of the ocean—the pulse of our liquid planet.

Fairfield, Iowa is the home of the Maharishi University. Two giant domes stand on the campus. There are two instead of one so that males and females can meditate separately. Fairfield is a typical, Mid-Western town. Wooden houses line the streets, all with front porches and backyards big enough for summer barbecues. Up until a few years ago, there was only one elevator in the entire town.

Traffic is obviously not a problem here, unless you are driving at the same time the populace is going to the domes. At 9:00 a.m. sharp, the first, two-hour meditation or "programming" session begins. The streets look as though every person in town jumped into their cars and headed up the hill. At 11:00 a.m., all the cars come back down. The parade of cars passes by again in the afternoon.

Fairfielders affectionately call themselves "tators," short for meditators. People have gathered from all over the world to set up residency near the university. They are the foundation of the transcendental meditation movement.

The leaders proclaim that when enough of their followers meditate on a particular problem, the problem disappears. Some groups in the transcendental movement have even put their services out to bidders around the country, like "new age" rainmakers.

When most people think of meditation, they think of sitting around for long periods of time, doing nothing, trying to think about nothing, waiting for some kind of divine inspiration. There are some who practice such meditation. Others meditate for even longer periods of time than the "tators." In fact, many give up all their worldly possessions, travel to some far off place and lose all contact with the physical world for years. Is this because they are more spiritual than others, or because they want to escape from life? Meditation is a practical art and a useful science. The purpose is not to drop out from the rest of us earthbound mortals, but to bring the answers you receive back to earth and use them for good.

The 12th century mystic, Meister Eckhart advised, "I've told this time and time again. If a person in a rapture as great as St. Paul once experienced, learned that her neighbor were in need of a cup of soup, it would be best to withdraw from the rapture and give that person the soup she needed."

Joel Goldsmith, a famous metaphysical thinker, was asked how long he meditated each day. His reply was, "I don't." What he meant was he didn't set aside a specific time each day as his time to meditate. He did admit, however, he connects with Spirit, many times a day. Joel Goldsmith is considered a mystic in the purest form of the term. Psychics, such as the ones on the infomercials, allegedly read people's thoughts. They have varying stories because they work in the subjective realm and physical energies. There is great competition amongst psychics. Mystics do not compete, because they all see one truth. They bring forth the same story because of their unity with the Divine. Therefore, mystics walk in a state of continual connectedness.

How are we to find this point of connection? Through the practice of meditation. This practice creates the space for a conscious connection of awareness, a time when you can consciously expand your understanding of the universe. It is finding oneness with the life energy. Dr. W. Brugh Joy called meditation, "...the journey to the everywhere of the entire universe...divinity's playground."

One form of meditation is not better than another. Whether you choose to sit in a giant dome with two hundred other meditators, or in a corner of your bedroom, you can reach that place of unity. What's important is to find what works for you and to take the time to consciously connect.

Everyone has experienced the meditative state at some time. Chris approached me after class and said, "My fiancé needs help. He tries to meditate but he can't."

I asked her, "Just out of curiosity, what does John do for a living?"

"Why he's a composer. He writes background music for movies."

I laughed and said, "Tell him he already meditates." The only way John the composer, or Michelangelo the artist can create something out of nothing is to tap into the spiritual realm for guidance.

## Pavarotti and Friends

Have you ever watched Luciano Pavorotti sing? He finishes the last note and the audience goes wild. But the audience begins applauding before Luciano knows his song is finished. At least two seconds pass before he even opens his eyes. If you look closely, you can see a definite shift in his posture and look. It's as though he isn't mentally conscious when he sings and then he comes back to the stage. The truth is he is in a meditative state, a state of connectedness. Paramahansa Yogananda writes, "Intuition is soul guidance, appearing naturally in man during those instances his mind is calm." Anything you do which doesn't involve your conscious thinking is a form of meditation.

For long distance runners, running is a meditation. After going 20 miles or more, if they were thinking clearly and consciously, they would probably stop, if not collapse. Slalom skiers, if fully conscious, would knock over the poles and tumble down the hills. While cooking her favorite meal, Mom is in a meditative state as she adds a pinch of this and a touch of that. Children playing video games hour after hour are not fully conscious. We all go into meditative states. We just don't recognize the practice as such. There have been many times when I've finished a talk and can't remember what I said because I had surrendered myself to Spirit.

The problem is most of us don't know how to consciously connect with that creative energy. Artists, dancers, musicians and athletes know how, but only after years of lessons and hours of practice do they allow themselves to surrender.

You can't overcome the ocean; you can only respect

it as you paddle out to participate in the joyous challenge of its waves. You can't overcome the great potential, but with respect it reveals itself to (and as) you.

Are you inwardly satisfied with your thoughts, feelings and personal behavior? You would do well to examine your inner condition through the practice of meditation.

I encourage my students to begin by taking some time to sit in the silence, or play soft, background music. New age, classical or any other sounds that soothe you work best. Find a portion of the day when you can regularly commit to taking this time for yourself. Twenty minutes is a good starting point.

When I first began meditating, I thought the early morning would be best for me. I set my alarm thirty minutes before I needed to get up. One corner of my room was designated my meditation spot. I'd wander sleepily, eyes still half closed, over to the corner. Within five minutes, I'd be fast asleep again. Next, I set aside time late at night. All the cares of the day were gone. There was nothing that needed doing. Unfortunately, I was too content, because the same thing happened. Less than five minutes into my meditation, my eyelids became too heavy to hold up and Christian was off to dreamland (not that it's a bad thing to go to sleep).

Now, each morning I walk down to the cliffs in front of my house in Del Mar, overlooking the Pacific Ocean. The cool breezes off the water and the quiet that permeates the scene allows me to shut off the rest of the world and open my mind to the Spirit. I set my daily work schedule to allow me time to do my meditation. At noon each day, I take half an hour to consciously connect. I tell my secretary, "Hold the calls. I'm in conference with God." No interruptions, no noise, no thoughts of having to be some-where else.

Find a time of day and a place that suits your schedule. Sit down in a suitable comfortable place. Get your body into a comfortable position, one you will be able to stay in for the twenty minutes. Don't do this on a full stomach, because your body will be focused on digesting.

Be there without judgment, expectations or rules. There is nothing to get, no right answers. You are just training yourself to receive your own intuitive thoughts. In other words, you want your mind to go past all of the world-ly concerns and reveal its true nature to you in the silence. "True silence," said William Penn, "is the rest of the mind. It is to the spirit what sleep is to the body, nourishment and refreshment." Our mission is to hear the news from the silence.

Ever try to clear your mind of all human thoughts, get it to be silent? You'll find the ego will step in, the "monkey mind," which says: "I have three more phone calls to return." "I'm hungry." "I forgot to take out the trash." "I'd rather be surfing." "Why are you wasting twenty minutes in the midst of your busy day? You could be accomplishing so much!" This is not the news of the silence we are listening for.

When you first begin, you'll probably think of a thousand things you'd rather do than sit still and simply experience the quiet. My meditation times were very short to begin with, but as I relaxed more, time passed more swiftly and my "monkey mind" quieted down.

The key to quieting down the random thoughts is to let them move through. It's as though everything that has gone on in your physical world is saved and stored as on a computer disk. Its job is to report all the data back to you. Once it gets you up to date, only the most current of information needs to be relayed.

After about a week of consistent time, you'll find a tiny gap where your mind stops bouncing around. The next day the gap may widen a bit. The following week, you may find a couple times when you experience pure space within your allocated twenty minutes. In this space is where Spirit can begin to reveal itself. As you practice meditation on a regular basis, the clear space without the "monkey mind" enlarges. You get to the place where you can almost clear the tabletop instantly. You can go there and immediately find the clearing, quiet your mind, ask a question and have it revealed to you—the insights from on high—all without closing your eyes.

**Tools of the Trade**

From the various meditation techniques, you will find what works best for you. Some people go into their meditations by concentrating on their breath. You may find this focuses your mind as well. Breathe in for seven seconds, then breathe out seven. Inhale seven seconds, exhale seven. The rhythm will draw you away from the physical world and into the ethereal.

Guided meditations, from a cassette tape or a live presenter, seem to work well for some people. This form of meditation will take you to a special, safe place, such as a forest, a beach or a meadow. You may be asked to visualize treasure chests loaded with gifts, dark caves that will take you deep into the earth, or heavenly staircases leading you to the gates of spirituality. For some people, listening to a voice giving specific directions, keeps their minds from wandering.

Focusing on objects, such as a candle, is another popular form of meditation. Crystals, pyramids or altars with pictures of an admired guru are also popular focal points. They serve the same purpose as rosary beads in Catholicism, a specific place to which your thoughts are drawn.

You may learn a mantra, a Hindu term for a word or phrase that is to be repeated. Many mantras are single words such as Om, peace, Shanti (peace in the Hindu language), or love. The idea of a mantra is to quiet your mind and focus your thoughts on God. My favorite is "I'm grateful."

Special places to mediate are great. You can find your quiet space anywhere. Some truth seekers believe there are "energy vortexes" in the world. Machu Picchu in Peru is said to be a good one. There is Mt. Shasta in California, Sedona, Arizona, and many others are located around the world. Going to one of these energy centers, you may really connect with Spirit. But what if you can't get there? If the exotic spot or sacred place is where you think you can find God, how can you connect when you're elsewhere? Can you reconnect in your backyard, or during rush hour on the freeway? You're probably going to spend more time there than on top of a mountain halfway across the world. Ernest Holmes, in his epic work The Voice Celestial, advised, "There is no need to leave the world of men, nor to retreat to some high cave or glen." Spirit is right where you are.

Once when I was sitting up on the cliffs, I was contemplating the beauty of the day. The rising sun was absolutely gorgeous. Pink clouds reflected its rays. All of a sudden, I almost felt myself floating with the clouds, as they traveled silently though the skies. I felt a oneness with the rolling waves of the ocean. My breathing felt in harmony with the ebb and flow of the tides. I noticed the grass rippling in the wind before me in the same rhythm as my breath. It all felt as if it were part of the same vibration. My body, the rocks and the wind were all breathing in sync with the ocean. This was an amazing sense of unity and connectedness. My individuality dropped away and I felt connected with all life. I wasn't trying to visualize prosperity, a soul mate or my perfect job. I had no expectations from my cliff walk that morning. I just knew, as Emerson said, "There is a principle which is the basis of things...simple, quiet, understated...we are not to do, but to let do, not to work, but be worked upon." Spirit had worked upon me. I was left with a sense of balance, harmony and fluidity. My mind, body and soul were part of the eternal flow of the universe.

What that means in a conscious state of mind is difficult to explain. But the moment did leave me with a deeper sense of interrelatedness to all nature. Anything that can give you a deeper feeling of relationship to Source must be constructive and positive for all humankind.

Included here are two guided meditations for your use. I suggest you record them in your own voice, pausing in appropriate places. Soft music playing in the background may assist you in capturing your attention. You'll find, each time you go through these meditations, you will reach a deeper level of relaxation and knowing.

### A Dream Wave

Get into a comfortable position, one where you

aren't going to want to move for 15-20 minutes. If possible, play some soothing, meditative music in the background. Breathe in for three counts, then hold for a count of three. Exhale for a beat of three, remain empty for three. Consciously repeat this cycle a few times until your mind seems clear.

Sense yourself walking down a canyon or dirt path. Notice the green, lush plants growing on the side. Feel the earth beneath your bare feet. Experience an ocean breeze against your face, coming up from the bottom of the canyon. Smell the salt air. Come to a place where the path opens up onto the beach. Notice the expansive, blue ocean with big waves peeling perfectly before you, as their white, foamy iridescence sparkles under the sun.

Feel the warm sand move beneath your feet as you walk up to a thatched roof hut. There is a tanned, old guardian who appears to know wise things but shares his insights in symbolic stories. He is known as the keeper of the watch. He asks you about your dreams and your fears. Take the next four minutes of time to ponder his question and relate the answers to him.

Now it's time to take a surfboard and face the fear—the big waves. Know the ride can bring great joy that will lead you to your ultimate dream.

You pick the perfect board and walk to the tide's edge. Feel the chill of the water on your feet, then dive onto your board, gliding easily across the water as you paddle out in the relatively calm channel. As you look over to the lineup, the place the waves are breaking, you feel excitement moving through your body. You move closer to where the action is taking place.

All of a sudden, you're paddling up the face of towering, mountainous waves, feeling as if you are going to be sucked backwards over some gigantic waterfall. As you speed down the other side of the wave, you notice one of your fears has come up. The wave in front of you has broken and a wall of white, turbulent water is coming straight towards you.

Rather than panic, you take the nose of the board and push it down, underneath the wall of foam. You experience the energy of that which you feared and allow it to pass over you.

You come to the surface revitalized, energized and feeling healthy. The next wave rolls in. You turn your board towards the shore and start paddling. You sense this is the one you've been waiting for. The wave catches up to your momentum. You are lifted high, towering into the sky. You look down the face of the wave and see the ocean below being drawn up into this rising mountain. You know that with the momentum you must decide to pull out or commit.

You take the last stroke to push yourself directly into your dream wave. You trust the process as you drop into the wave. You are now part of life's momentum. You direct the powerful energy as you glide to the bottom of the wave and make a turn with ease. With the energy life is giving you, you look up the face of this wave and feel a composure. You are one with the power. You move with grace and strength to the top of the wave and back down again.

You experience great exhilaration as the crest of the wave, the lip, begins to fold over your head. You find yourself in a perfect, blue barrel of moving water. There is such a powerful sound it fills the room where you're sitting right now. It will take you to the place of knowing you can accomplish anything. Go back and ask yourself again, "What is my dream?" (Take five minutes to answer fully.)

Now feel yourself being blown out of this blue room and gently riding down the shoulder of the wave, then stepping back onto the beach with heightened awareness and a conscious willingness to bring this renewed sense back with you. So slowly and gently come back to your body.

## A Magic Carpet Ride

Close your eyes. Take three deep breaths. Inhale...exhale...in...out...in...out. Now we're going to go through the muscles of your body, tighten and release them, one by one. As you release the tension in each muscle, you go deeper into the realm of Spirit.

Begin with your toes. Tighten them, hold for two counts, then relax. Do the same with your ankles then your calves, your thighs, then buttocks and hips. Move to the chest area, your back, shoulders, arms and hands. Hold all of these places of tension for two counts, then relax.

In this place of relaxation, the final release, slip into that place where you have let go of the tension from your outer world. Go where your thoughts want to take you. Mentally hover above your body. Feel yourself being lifted to a higher state of awareness. In this lifting, I invite you to come to a beautiful green meadow. The grass is blowing with the wind. Smell the freshness of the outdoors. Stroll joyfully through the high grass. See an oak tree in the distance. Hear the birds singing and look for the deer watching you through the bushes.

Under the oak tree is a beautiful Oriental rug. Sit down, cross-legged. Get into the place where you are fully relaxed. The deer walks up to you and nuzzles its nose against your ear and licks your face. Feel the cool, dampness and accept the love of nature. Be aware of the abundance of your environment.

As you sit there, feel the rug moving beneath you. Notice that it's beginning to lift you above the ground. You realize you've been sitting on a magic carpet, rising higher and higher into the sky. Feel the breeze against your face, your hair blowing in the wind.

Now the carpet is floating through the clouds. From the elevated perspective, you can see your life. Look upon your life for the next 5-10 minutes, without judgment. Be aware of what comes into your mind over these next few minutes, as you go to an even deeper level of consciousness . . .

You and your magic carpet float gently back to earth and settle to the ground underneath the oak tree. Know that anytime you wish, you can climb aboard this magic carpet and drift to a higher state of understanding and awareness. You have brought back a conscious understanding of the insights you just gained. You are now back in the room, into your body. Be here now, refreshed, rejuvenated, revitalized and ready to move forward into the new day.

*Eleven*

# Epilogue

*The physical body is but a vehicle,*
*a marvelous instrument granted us*
*for a brief time. Such form is necessary for*
*us to express life on this particular plane.*
*When the life within us has reached*
*the point where it no longer needs*
*the physical body, it leaves.*
*As the eagle freed from the cage*
*soars to its native heights, so the soul*
*of us all, when freed*
*from its temporary home of flesh,*
*rises and returns unto the Father's house,*
*naked and unafraid.*

# Chapter 11

# EPILOGUE

**You Are Immortal**

Deep in thought, I sat on the bluff, contemplating the majestic waves of the ocean before me. Traveling across her surface, those waves spanned the horizon to rise up in their glorious expression of energy—only to crash and die upon the shore. Yet as I sat and watched them, I clearly saw how they each returned to her—the ocean, their source—to express once again . . .

That morning, one of my lifelong buddies called me with news of one of our friends. Earlier in the year, he moved with his wife and two children to Arizona. "We want to get away from the earthquakes," he told me at the time. Now choking back tears my buddy informed me our friend was riding an ATV over the weekend and got thrown off. He broke his neck and was killed. Sobbing, he asked, "What can I say to his wife and children to make it better?"

"There is nothing you can say to make it better," I answered, "just love them and be there for them."

How does the word "death" feel to you? Are you comfortable with the concept, or does it put chills up your spine?

My grandmother taught me many great lessons. One was the comfort she gave me around the process of death. Cancer had taken over her body and the doctors pronounced her "incurable." Seven years later, when the cancer magically disappeared, they had to admit it was a remission. Grandma lived several years longer, but finally succumbed to a stroke. She and begun the recovery process, even to the point of getting her speech back, but ultimately she seemed to lose the desire and drive to carry on with her life.

I knew in my heart that making the transition from life to death was a conscious decision on her part. Before Grandma left, she made sure all her affairs were in order. At her request, we called for a Catholic priest, since Catholicism was the religion she followed. Surrounded by those she loved, Grandma said her "good-byes" and made her transition. It was Christmas morning. My mom said, "Your grandmother gave us the greatest Christmas present she could have given." For me, next to birthday presents, Christmas presents were the greatest thing around. To think of death in this way was a beautiful gift. I was able to watch the process of death in my home and learn it was natural. The experience stands vividly out in my mind, right next to bringing my baby brother home from the hospital. One was birth; one was death—the two most profound occurrences of life.

**The River of Life**

We were heading toward Pashupatináth, one of the sacred Hindu temples at the headwaters of the Ganges River. It was sunrise when we came up to a dirt road. As the mist began to rise, the sun shone over the golden spirals of the temple. You could feel life starting to unfold. People were bathing or washing their clothes in the river. Others went to the temple to pray.

My eyes caught sight of two people carrying what looked to be a lifeless body. They built a funeral pyre from pieces of wood that lay on the banks of the river. The youngest boy began to prepare his mother's corpse. He oiled down the body and then lit her mouth. The lighting of that portion of her body represented the last purification of the physical form. The fire represented a moving toward the spiritual light.

I watched, captivated by the event. Below, children played in the river, hardly noticing what was happening. "How strange," I thought. What later came to my mind was the boy was taking care of his mother's physical body just as we clean the closets after a loved one dies. The clothes are no longer useful, nor is the body.

Annie Besant, Second President of the Theosophical Society said, "Man is essentially a Spirit...in a body of very subtle matter, life cannot work without a body of some kind...the body is often therefore spoken of as a vehicle, that which carries the life..." The Bhagavad-Gita likens man's body to an overcoat, saying, just because a man puts on an overcoat to go outside, doesn't mean he is the overcoat. We are housed within physical bodies, but we are not the body.

I've talked over the idea of death with scientists, theologians, medical doctors and philosophers. The beliefs they hold are not necessarily peculiar to one profession. Rather, they are personal in nature. Some believe in an afterlife, others in heaven and hell. What I share with you is what I believe to be true. There isn't any place you can prove my theories, for they are personal as well.

To begin with, we need to get rid of the belief that we are only human beings, for we are spiritual beings on this human plane. We are unlimited potential, far greater than this physical body. Our spiritual body extends so far, vast and wide; it cannot be what's crammed into this physical thing called body. Yet, instead of God consciousness, we get caught up in the physical sensations. Beyond the physical we are always connected to God, Spirit, everlasting life. This concept is imprinted at the deepest level of our being.

Some people have spent long years agonizing over the concept and fear of death. Yet death as an end does not exist. Only the physical body dies. Paul says, "We die daily." That means we let go of old ideas daily. We may change jobs, residences, schools, or lose friends to relocation. These are all deaths we experience daily. The change that occurs around them allows birth to take place, which is the beginning of something greater in life.

The two concepts that surround the idea of death are fear and tragedy. As we get to a greater realization of this concept at the heart level, we need not fear death. And when we no longer fear death, there will no longer be tragedy. There is no need to fear death, for we are immortal. But we don't have to die to become immortal—we simply are immortal.

To lose a dear friend or relative after years of loving and sharing is terribly painful. It is difficult to part with such a positive force in your life. In reality, we never lose the people we love. They continue to live in our hearts and minds. Their presence is felt in our every act, idea and decision. To quote Ernest Holmes, "A true realization of immortality and the continuity of the soul, will rob our grief of hopelessness."

The ancient philosopher, Homer, calls sleep "death's sister." He suggests that dying is like forgetting all the woes and troubles. Plato comments, "Birth is a sleeping and forgetting, death, an awakening and remembrance." Socrates was convinced that death was "the release of the soul from the chains of the body."

The physical body is but a vehicle, a marvelous instrument granted us for a brief time. Such form is necessary for us to express life on this particular plane. When the life within us has reached the point where it no longer needs the physical body, it leaves. As the eagle freed from the cage soars to its native heights, so the soul of us all, when freed from its temporary home of flesh, rises and returns unto the Father's house, naked and unafraid.

Our loved ones are forever in God's keeping. They are safe. Loving friends have met them and their life still flows on the currents of eternity. Let us feel that we have not lost them. They have simply gone before us, our ambassadors on the other side.

## A New Adventure

It is the people left behind who experience death as tragedy. It's okay and natural to grieve at the loss of a loved one. We feel we're missing a part of who we are. But it's also natural for the grieving process to end. When we get caught up in "woe is me," we send out negative vibrations that do not allow this soul to be free. We believe we are holding their hands, but in reality we are chaining their souls. As a ship needs to be freed from its mooring, we must allow our loved ones to begin their new adventure.

Several people, who were revived after being pronounced clinically dead, shared with me how beautiful the death experience was. In Embraced by the Light, Betty Eadie did not want to leave "that glorious world of light and love for one hardship and uncertainty," but realized she was still needed on earth. Often the pain of the tragedy of the people left behind is too great to bear for those who have crossed over. They say they consciously make the decision to experience their physical pain and come back rather than put their loved ones through the tragic experience of loss.

People, who have crossed over and come back, suddenly have an unshakable conviction the soul continues. You can tell them their experience was a hallucination, but they know better. They begin to integrate the event into their lives and no longer worry about death.

Many hover over their bodies in the hospital room, aware of every thought in the room. Some speak of a whirling, buzzing sound that's not audible, but they know it's there. They move through a dark tunnel towards a bright light that somehow beckons them. Several have a panoramic, 3D, living color vision of their lives, but not in a sequential manner. Some will even say every thought they ever thought they watched unfold before them. They can now see the consequences of those thoughts in an omniscient way. (I know I'm in trouble if this is true. In fact, we may all be in trouble!)

There's a loving figure and familiar faces to assist them. They say it's not a presence they can actually see, but one they feel. Loving hands greet us there at birth. Why shouldn't there be the same loving hands on the other side?

### We're Glad You're Back

Dan Covey, one of the members of my congregation at Seaside Church, related his near death experience to me. Fifteen years ago, Dan was diagnosed with

Parkinson's disease. One of the many symptoms is uncontrollable tremors.

In 1987, at Parkland Hospital in Dallas, Texas, Dan underwent experimental surgery to alleviate his tremors. He was the first patient of Dr. Clarke, a prominent neurosurgeon at the hospital. The team of surgeons removed Dan's left adrenal gland and placed it in the medulla portion of the brain. This gland naturally secretes a chemical similar to Dopamine. A deficiency of Dopamine causes the tremors.

The operation, which was considered successful, lasted from 6:00 a.m. to 2:00 p.m. Following the surgery, Dan was taken to the intensive care unit. At approximately 8:00 p.m. his entire system shut down.

"I just checked out and hovered over my bed, right at the ceiling. I heard everything the doctors said as they did their heart massage and CPR. The next thing I knew, I was floating down a dark, tube-like tunnel. At first everything was completely dark. I had no sense of time whatsoever. A light at the end of the tunnel caught my attention. It was at least ten times brighter than looking directly at the sun, but it didn't hurt my eyes. Focused only on that beam of light, I couldn't see anything else.

"I reached the opening and met people I recognized—not in bodies like ours, but a familiar energy. My dad, who had passed over ten years earlier, was there. So were my late grandfather and my infant son, who died at six-months-old. We had matters to settle between all of us, petty grievances, resentments, and misunderstandings. When we finished, love was the only thing remaining.

"There was an energy about me, giving me the choice to go back to earth or stay in the light. I made the decision to come back in order to teach other people how to love. Prior to my experience, I had been an angry, Type-A personality in a high stress job. I showed no affection to those I loved. Now was the opportunity to make up for the years I lost and the love I missed. By the time I regained consciousness, I had been clinically dead for sixteen minutes.

"I don't remember coming back. The next thing I heard was Dr. Clarke saying, 'Dan, you scared us.' I felt confused about what had happened. I wasn't even sure it had been real, because it didn't fit into my earthly thinking processes. After about six months, I was able to remember bits and pieces and acknowledge my experience as real. Although I'm not sure I want to relive the experience, I now know it was one of the most incredible, life changing events of my life."

## An Emerging Consciousness

Everyday there is greater awareness and growing acceptance of the experience called "death" coming to our consciousness. Judging from the number of books being written on the subject, people seem to be more curious than ever before.

Writers like Dr. Raymond Moody and his book, Life After Life, generated great interest. His works was close to the beginning of mass interest over the subject. Reading it made me wonder why and if near death experiences just began occurring in the last decade or two. My research told this phenomenon was not new. We are simply more open to listening. Maybe we're finally ready to let go of our misconceptions about the process of death.

Samuel Taylor Coleridge, the 19th century poet,

proposed the question of coming back from death way back then: "What if you slept? And what if, in your sleep, you dreamed? And what if, in your dream, you went to heaven and plucked a beautiful flower? And what if, when you awoke, you had the flower in your hand? Ah, then what?" Even further back in history the subject was broached, but not broadly explained. The last story in Plato's Republic told of a famous warrior who had died. A team of embalmers had the corpse on the table, preparing it for the burial. Suddenly, the warrior sat straight up. Everyone went, "Wow!" (or its equivalent in those days). What the warrior had to share in this story has an uncanny similarity to the death experience of today.

The important book, Cosmic Consciousness by Richard Bucke, came out at the turn of the century. He wrote, "The illumination of this experience, this fear of death which haunts so many men and women at some time falls off like an old cloak. Not, however, as a result of reason, it simply vanishes. That person knows without learning that the universe is not a dead machine but a loving presence. That person understands what the scripture says: We live and move and have our being in Him."

## Many Mansions

Jesus said, "In my Father's house are many rooms. If it were not so, I would have told you." By "many rooms," he meant many levels of consciousness. How many more rooms may there be in this mansion in addition to this plane of existence? We get caught up in wanting God to leave us on this level forever. Life doesn't work this way. We're expanding, growing and sometimes we need the nudge to leave the room, so the body drops away.

When this body is gone, another body appears. We are travelers of the universe. Yet, the place to travel is within. This is the place we need to explore—to discover our greater selves.

Dr. Ernest Holmes, in the Science of Mind text-book, writes, "There are bodies within bodies to infinity." In Words that Heal Today, he says, "There are bodies here and there are bodies there." The apostle Paul said, "There are bodies celestial and there are bodies terrestrial."

The story goes, Jesus appeared after physical death to show us individual life goes on. At the time death was the greatest fear to man. Times have not changed much. We must destroy this irrational fear. He showed us this plane of existence is not the last. We're not absorbed and returned back to some massive energy. No sequence is broken. Life is like a strip of film, with this awareness being only one frame. We carry our consciousness with us across the borderline of this plane of life to the next. One plane reproduces itself on another—the Hermetic philosophy of: "As above, so beneath. As below, so above." Things in the physical world are copies of those that are in heaven. Things that are seen are the same as those that are unseen. There is something more than this physical body and we are far greater. We might as well accept this now. Like it or not, this truth is something we're going to have to deal with eventually.

Let us come to a comfortable realization of death in our life. When we do, we'll experience an inner peace. Ironically, the acceptance of death will make us more alive than ever before. Know death does not extinguish life. It has no power over life, just as darkness has no power over light.

Catch the Spirit
1613 Lake Dr.
Encinitas, CA 92024
(760)753-5786

Date Printed: 09/05/2010
Store: 1 Date: 09/05/2010
Register: 1-3 Time: 12:25:23 PM
Receipt: RC00001000018577
Tran type: Sale
Cashier: Karis

| UPC | DESCRIPTION | |
|---|---|---|
| SZ SUBSZ COLR | QTY @ PRICE | SUBTTL |
| 400100004814 | CATCH/SPIRIT RIDING | |
| N/A N/A | 1 @ 11.95 | 11.95 |

| | SubTotal | 11.95 |
|---|---|---|
| | Total Tax | 1.05 |
| | Total | 13.00 |

Total # of Items: 1

Balance 0.00

All returns must be within 30 days of
sale with store reciept.

Immortality is either a principle of nature, or it doesn't exist. Everyone is immortal, or no one is. The near death experiences reported by ordinary people as well as Yogis have proven life is eternal and the individuality of the soul continues. If we believe the examples not the exceptions, then we are immortal.

Begin to surrender the fear of losing the physical. There is nothing to fear when you choose life. Let go of the fear of not being. You shall always be. You will never lose; instead, you will find your real self. How can you be less if your thoughts focus on being more? How can you die if you know that life is eternal?

I share the following story by the world-renowned author, Anonymous, at memorial services. My hope is that it gives you peace of mind about the concept of death and letting go.

I am standing on the seashore. A ship at my side spreads her white sails to the morning breeze and starts for the blue ocean. She is the object of beauty and strength. I watch her until, at length, she hangs like a speck of white cloud, just where the sea and the sky mingle with each other. Then someone at my side says, "There, she's gone." "Gone where?" I wonder.

Gone from my sight, that is all. She is just as large in mast and sail and spar as when she left my side. And she is just as able to bear her living weight to her destined port. Her diminished size is in me, not in her.

At the exact moment someone says, "There, she's gone," there are other eyes watching her coming. Other voices are ready to take the glad shout, "There she comes!" And that is dying.

## The Gathering

The crew comes together. Upon arriving at the parking lot, I take my surfboard from the top of the car. There is a collective knowingness that there has been a completion in the physical realm. It is a time to honor a dear friend. It is a time to remember with joy the support the friend offered in times of surfing wipeouts, personal trials and tribulations. I can clearly remember his voice encouraging me, "Go back out, Christian. You can do it!" I walk slowly down to the beach and hook up with the other members of my surfing family, the clan. There are people who haven't seen each other for years. Yet a real closeness still exists, because there is a task, unspoken yet understood, uniting everyone. The mood is solemn. No one has said a word. An occasional hug is offered and returned. A dear friend has gone on to be an ambassador in the cosmic waves, the celestial realm.

When the timing seems right, I put my flower lei around my neck, pick up my board and jump into the water. Dozens of people follow. They stretch through the waves, out into the sea. Silently, we paddle out past the breakers, past the turbulence. There we pull into a circle. We are ready to begin.

I toss my flower lei into the middle of the circle. Soon its center is filled with beautiful orchids. It is a time to share stories of history created together, joyful recollections. Some, like me, share only silence, remembering inwardly. It is in the silence that the Great Spirit touches everyone in the crew. There comes an inner realization that this completion is part of the full cycle, a closing of the chapter. It is the ending of a particular frame in the many frames of spiritual evolvement.

A wave crashes upon the beach and its energy dissipates, but is not gone. The energy released from the wave still exists, transformed into a new form of expression. I realize my friend has transformed into his new expression. Though the wave crashes, it has lost nothing; it is still part of the sea. This is the gathering. It is a deep understanding of an end, but also a realization of a new beginning.

The soul has been released from its mortal flesh. A physical body no longer exists. But Spirit animated the form, encouraged it to ride the waves of this planet, brought a twinkle to the eye, and inspired the voice to hoot and holler as it cruised through life. And Spirit is what carries on now, forever and ever.

# Catch the Spirit
# Riding the Waves of Life

## by Christian Sørensen

**Typefaces:**
Bodoni Book for Text, Gill Sans and Garamond
for Titles and Sub-Text.

**Second Edition**
Published, January, 2001

For information on additional public          ..apes, to schedule
personal appearances or to cor          .cate with the author,
please          .t:

## Cele     ..i Winds

1155 Carr  .o del Mar, PMB 411
D   Mar, CA 92014
]   x: 760 753-7647
E-Ma   ccs@seasidechurch.org